A The Canadian doption Guide

A Family at Last

Judith Wine

McGraw-Hill Ryerson
Toronto   Montreal

1 2 3 4 5 6 7 8 9 10 BBM 4 3 2 1 0 9 8 7 6 5

3220

First published in 1995 by
McGraw-Hill Ryerson Limited
300 Water Street
Whitby, Ontario, Canada
L1N 9B6

Publisher: Donald S. Broad

Family Circus cartoon reprinted with the special permission of King Features Syndicate.

Canadian Cataloguing in Publication Data

Wine, Judith
  A family at last : a Canadian guide to finding
and adopting your child

Includes bibliographical references and index.
ISBN 0-07-551820-1

1. Adoption – Canada. I. Title.

HV875.58.C2W5 1994   362.7'34'0971   C94-931654-7

This publication is designed to provide accurate and authoritative information on the subject matter covered. Laws are constantly changing, and the examples given are intended to be general guidelines only.

This book is sold on the understanding that neither the author nor the publisher is engaged in rendering legal, accounting or other professional advice. If legal advice or other expert assistance is required, the services of a competent professional should be sought.

Author photo: David Amoils
Cover design: Dianna Little
Photo courtesy of Telegraph Colour Library/Masterfile
Editorial services provided by Word Guild, Markham, Ontario

Printed in Canada

For the two most important people in my life:
my husband, Mitch, and my son, Brady.
And for Debbie, whose courage gave me a son.

Acknowledgements

There are many people who helped make this book a reality. I gratefully acknowledge their assistance.

First, there are the adoptive parents who shared their stories so that you and I could learn. Their experiences shaped the information and advice set out in this book.

Katherin Jones and Robin Hilborn, the editor and publisher of the Toronto newsletter *Adoption Helper*, graciously agreed to let us use data that took them many years to gather. This data—contact information for adoptive parent support groups and adoption organizations, newsletters and magazines—forms the basis of Appendices I and II.

Various government adoption professionals provided essential aid by reviewing the legal summary for their provinces: Keith Owen and Sherry Glanville (Alberta), Jeannette Carlson (British Columbia), Donna Dickson (Manitoba), Nicole Richard and Dick Quigg (New Brunswick), Rosemary Atherton (Newfoundland), Mary Beauchamp (Northwest Territories), Susan M. Drysdale (Nova Scotia), Gail Moffatt (Ontario), Virginia MacEachern (Prince Edward Island), Anne-Marie Fleurant (Quebec), Gerald E. Jacob (Saskatchewan), and Maxine Kehoe (Yukon Territory).

Numerous other adoption professionals contributed needed information and explanations: Cheryl Appell (Dickson, Sachs, Appell & Beaman: Toronto), Dale Briggs (Stewart & Cooper: Moncton), Terry Hodgskin (Barr, Wensel, Nesbitt, Reeson: Edmonton), Christine Johnson (Soleil des Nations: Trois-Rivières), Carol Lavelle (Adoption Agency & Counselling Service: Burlington), Joyce Masselink (Choices Adoption & Counselling Services: Victoria), Marilyn Shinyei (Adoption Options: Edmonton) and Phil Yang (National Adoption Desk: Ottawa).

Finally, there are my family and friends who provided endless encouragement and patience. They had the difficult task of living with me while I wrote this book. Three family members deserve special mention. Shelly Greisman, my mother, who gave me the freedom to write by lovingly caring for my son two days a week for almost two years. Esther Wine, my other mother, who provided assistance and enthusiasm whenever needed. And Mitchell Wine, my husband, whose support for my dream, tolerance of the resulting inconveniences and thoughtful critique of every written word (including this acknowledgement) were invaluable.

Thank you.

Contents

Introduction

This book was written for people just like my husband and me. Not as we are now, but as we were several years ago. It is the book that we looked for when we first considered adoption as the means of creating our family.

By June of 1991, my husband and I were finally ready to stop pursuing a medical solution to our childlessness. Even thinking about further medical intervention drove us into a state of depression. It was only when we talked about adoption that we felt any hope or excitement. We decided to begin the adoption process.

After several telephone calls, I found the appropriate government sponsored agency. I first asked about the necessary procedures. I then asked the question that would change our lives: how long would it take to adopt? The answer was devastating: seven years.

Although I did not realize it until much later, we were lucky. The adoption professional I reached understood my question and the importance of receiving a succinct answer. She realized that we, like most prospective parents, were picturing a healthy newborn who looked somewhat like us. She knew that we needed to understand that our chances of adopting such a child through the government were slim. Her answer told us that we must change either the mental image of our child or our method of adoption.

After wandering around in a state of despair for several days, I decided to investigate our alternatives. I visited libraries and stores looking for a book that would point us in the right direction. I did not find one. Although I found several helpful American books, it became apparent that the Canadian situation was different.

Again we were lucky. A friend knew a couple who had recently adopted a child. The couple kindly agreed to share their experiences with us. They explained private adoption—the alternative to working with the government or a government-sponsored agency—and described how it worked in our province. They gave us the names of other adoptive parents and of adoption professionals who could help. They started us on our way.

The next few months were spent learning and working. We learned about the adoption world and how to search for our child ourselves. We worked hard at searching until, in March of 1992, our son was born.

Months later when it was our turn to share our knowledge, I was reminded of the anguish of not having a written source of assistance. I cannot imagine what we would have done had we not found help elsewhere. This book is my response.

* * *

The book is divided into three parts. The first part introduces the adoption world. Comprehensive information is provided about everything from making the decision to adopt to creating an adoption plan. The adoption alternatives are explained. The legal rules and steps of each province and territory are outlined.

The focus then narrows to the adoption alternative that worked for us—a Canadian private adoption. Part II explains how prospective adoptive parents may search for their child themselves. Step-by-step instructions are provided on the necessary preparations and the numerous ways to search.

The final part of the book helps put everything together. Practical advice is offered on how to survive the time between finding and adopting the child. Issues that are faced after the adoption are discussed.

A personal essay and three appendices complete the book. The personal essay, *Tears for My Son*, shares the emotional turmoil my husband and I survived during our adoption experience. The appendices set out information about hundreds of adoptive parent support groups and adoption organizations, newsletters, books and studies.

* * *

This book contains the information that my husband and I sought during our adoption experience. I hope it provides what you (or your friend or your client or whomever) need. However, since every journey is different, the knowledge required is often different. You will surely discover something of interest that has not been discussed. Please share your thoughts with me (contact information is in Appendix I) so that, in future editions, I may share them with others.

I have addressed this book to couples considering adoption because an infertility or medical condition is preventing them from becoming parents by birth. Most of the information is also relevant to single prospective adoptive parents and those who are motivated to adopt by feelings of altruism or social commitment.

I want to end this beginning with a few words for those of you who are prospective adoptive parents. I know where you are and where you have been—I have been there. It hurts. Sometimes it seems too difficult to go on. Do not give up. You have the necessary determination or you would not even be thinking about reading this book. Never lose sight of your goal. Work through the obstacles one at a time. Learn and work until you are successful. It is worth it. I promise.

Judith Wine
September, 1994

Part I
The Adoption World

10-22

©1993 Bil Keane, Inc.
Dist. by Cowles Synd., Inc.

"We came from Mommy's
tummy. But Joseph is adopted,
so he came from his
mommy's heart."

chapter ··················· 1

Deciding to Adopt

Adoption. A word you never thought would apply to your family. Yet now you are faced with the possibility of it being the best way to create that family.

For some people, there is no hesitation. Adoption is simply the next step. They cannot have a biological child; they are going to adopt a child.

If you are like most people, the path you must follow is not that clear. You do not immediately embrace adoption as the solution to your problem. You may have given up on medical science, or medical science on you, and yet cannot bring yourself to accept adoption. More likely, you are in the midst of your own make-a-baby treadmill, still holding on to the hope that the next attempt will work. However, you can no longer ignore the depression each failure brings. You are beginning to realize that you need to consider other alternatives.

In determining whether adoption is a viable alternative, there are two major issues you should explore. The first issue involves your infertility; the second, your attitude towards adoption.

Exploring these issues means reviewing the information presented in this book and then doing whatever is necessary to make yourself comfortable with either accepting or rejecting the adoption alternative. For some people, this will mean talking it over with their spouse. For others, additional research and detailed discussions with extended family, friends (old and new) and professional counsellors will also be necessary.

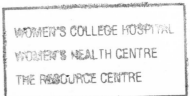
3

Dealing with Your Infertility

Infertility is a devastating crisis. It destroys our most sacred assumption—an assumption held by almost everybody since childhood. We expect to grow up, meet the man or woman of our dreams, get married, have kids and live happily ever after. Well, we grew up, met that special person, said "I do" and then our world turned upside down.

It is not surprising that many feel a loss of self-worth or self-esteem. Society has never accepted deviations from the norm and suddenly our life is not normal. We must learn how to cope with our new reality.

Potential Losses

In her books, *Taking Charge of Infertility*[1] and *Adopting after Infertility*,[2] Patricia Irwin Johnston outlines six distinct losses that infertility may cause:

- the loss of control over many aspects of life
- the loss of individual genetic continuity and an unbroken family blood line
- the loss of the joint conception of a child with one's life partner
- the loss of the physical satisfactions of pregnancy and birth
- the loss of the emotional gratifications of a shared pregnancy, birth and breast-feeding experience
- the loss of the opportunity to parent.

It is the possibility of one or more of these losses that are causing the anger, frustration and grief you are feeling. The losses, and the resulting emotions, must be addressed and your infertility accepted before you can move ahead with your life.

Adopting a child does not deal with all of these losses. It does allow you to parent a child. It may also, as you will learn, help you regain some control over your life. If these are the potential losses that you feel most deeply, adopting a child may be the answer for you. If not, you may need to look elsewhere.

Tears for My Son, an essay about the emotional side of my adoption experience can be found at the end of the book. It contains the following thoughts on the consequences of my infertility:

My son and I are not biologically related. So what. There is also no genetic connection with the other most important person in my life, my husband.

We would have wanted our child to have my husband's sense of humour and my nose. He would surely have had my sense of humour and my husband's nose. Since we have no expectations, there can be no disappointments, only excitement at the possibilities. Two tone-deaf parents may even have a musically gifted son.

Our son is a joint effort—from the moment he was first imagined, through finding and caring for him, to helping him learn to take care of himself. No one could convince me that I do not have a child conceived with my chosen life partner.

I would have liked to experience a *normal* pregnancy and birth. At least, I think I would. Yet, we did have our own child creating experiences. Someone once said that the process of adopting was "the longest labour on record." The difficulty of our labour brought us closer. It made us realize the strength of our commitment to each other and to having a family.

You must examine how you feel—which losses would cause you the most pain. You must also understand how your spouse feels. Then together you must devise a plan that will allow you both to (i) avoid as many painful losses as possible, and (ii) cope with the pain of any losses that cannot be avoided.

Do not expect this process to be easy. First, you are attempting to deal with potential losses while immersed in emotions caused by the thought of those losses. Recognize that stress is inherent in the process. Allow yourself as much time as you need.

Second, you and your spouse will probably have different views on the importance of each loss as well as on how to avoid or cope with it. You may even disagree on how to discuss those differing views.

My husband and I drove each other crazy. He wanted to discuss our problems all the time. I wanted to avoid them completely. Compromising was painful, but necessary.

Developing Your Survival Plan

My husband and I did not have any trouble devising a plan to deal with our infertility. From the start, there was one jointly accepted fact: we were going to be parents. It was understood that we would not give up until our desire had become a reality.

We did not think in terms of *plans* or *losses*. I had not begun to feed my appetite to read and learn. Yet without realizing what we were doing, we followed a plan that reflected our views about the potential losses. We first attempted to use the marvels of medical science to assist us in having a biological child. When we could no longer cope with the treatments and the resulting disappointments, we started to consider adoption—an alternative that avoided the one loss we could not accept.

If you and your spouse are having trouble developing your plan, you may wish to contact an infertility organization (see Appendix I for contact information). Such organizations, and their adoption counterparts, can be very helpful. They provide support, answer questions, steer you towards information seminars and supply names of helpful reference materials and professionals.

Reading either one of Johnston's books mentioned above, *Taking Charge of Infertility* or *Adopting after Infertility*, should prove very helpful. Johnston gives practical advice on issues such as the angst of being the less fertile spouse, resolving an impasse between spouses and dealing with family and friends. I was surprised at how much of my journey was contained in her discussions. Also interesting is Linda Salzer's *Surviving Infertility: A Compassionate Guide through the Emotional Crisis of Infertility*.[3]

Pursuing Adoption

If you decide that adoption is a viable alternative, your plan must include some sense of when you are going to start the process. We did not start until we had decided that emotionally we could no longer continue our attempts to have a biological child. I did not feel capable of enthusiastically following both alternatives at the same time.

Until recently, this was the only acceptable way to pursue adoption. In other words, it was thought that before a couple was ready to adopt a child, they must have resolved their infertility by accepting they would not have a biological child.

Kerry J. Daly, who co-directed the 1993 National Adoption Study with Michael P. Sobol,[4] examined this issue in his 1987 Ph.D. thesis.[5] His research led him to conclude that while this approach was true for some infertile couples, for others, there could be a concurrent commitment to both biological and adoptive parenthood.

It appears that this is a practical necessity of the times. Medical improvements have meant that infertility treatments can drag on for years, since there is almost no end to the techniques an infertile couple may try. Yet adopting a child can take years because shifts in society's values have meant there are fewer newborns available for adoption.

Not surprisingly, some couples conclude that their best chance to parent is to pursue both avenues simultaneously. They continue with medical treatments and the adoption process until they have a child.

Daly found that such couples can successfully pursue adoption. The couples resolve their infertility by accepting that they may or may not become biological parents, and by realizing that what is important is that they become parents.

What does all this mean? It seems to mean that you are ready to adopt a child when you have a positive attitude towards adoption, when it seems right to you. You must be ready to learn, excited at the possibilities. You no longer must accept the failure of one method of building a family, but rather be willing and ready to consider a new method of building.

Adoption—A Positive Way to Build a Family

"Her adopted daughter" rather than simply "her daughter." "How could his *real* parents give up so beautiful a child?" "Too bad you couldn't have any kids of your own." Comments that are made every day by well-meaning people. Comments that reflect society's attitude that a family created by adoption is somehow second-best.

Even if you have managed to stay untainted by this attitude, how—you are wondering—can you ignore the years you have just spent trying to have a biological child? Must you conveniently forget that adopting a child was not your first choice? Is that what is meant by a positive attitude towards adoption?

No. Adoption may be our second choice as a means of creating our families. That does not mean that our families are second-best. Adoptive parents' children are *theirs* with the same passion and ferocity that biological parents feel. They may wish that they had shared the birth experience with their children, but they do not want other children, by birth or otherwise. Adoptive parents feel—no, they *know*—that their children are the children they were meant to parent.

Having a positive attitude simply means still feeling confident about the idea of forming your family by adoption after you understand what the adoption experience entails. The adoption experience includes both the mechanics of adopting a child and the realities of parenting that child.

This book is about the mechanics—the adoption process. You still need to examine the issues involved in parenting an adopted child. Why, you are wondering, do you need to consider this now? You would much rather spend your time learning about the process. It hurts to think about raising a child you do not have. You'll worry about raising the kid when, and if, you finally get one. The only problem with this thought progression is that you need to understand what it means to get that child *by adoption*.

Parenting an adopted child is different from parenting a biological child. You need to be sure that you can accept and deal with those differences, that you can help your child deal with them. You also need to be sure that your family, friends and community can deal with the differences, or that you can handle those issues as well.

Do not misunderstand. Most of your parenting experiences will be the same as everyone else's. And just like everyone else, no matter how much you read before becoming parents, you will be unprepared for the experiences. So why do you need to be concerned with a few more unprepared experiences? Because those experiences are not what everyone else will have. Because you and your child may resent those abnormal experiences if not acknowledged as different. Because it is now realized that adoptive families suffer if they do not recognize and accept those differences.

What kind of differences are we talking about? Well, any possible consequence of the fact that your child was not born to you.

Your child may be noticeably different from you—physically, emotionally, mentally. She may have spent part of her life without you, possibly in an unhealthy environment. Her cultural background may be vastly different from your own. You may have no or negative information about her genetic background. Your child may want to learn about her genetic and cultural background—search out biological relatives, immerse in a different culture. Her biological parents may want to stay in contact with her and you. Some people will not consider your family *real*.

You may immediately feel confident about dealing with such differences in an open and positive fashion. If your spouse feels the same, move on. More likely, you will have a few concerns.

Take the time to examine those concerns. Discuss the issues with knowledgeable friends or professionals or glance at books such as Lois Melina's *Raising Adopted Children: A Manual for Adoptive Parents*;[6] Judith Schaffer and Christina Lindstrom's *How to Raise an Adopted Child*;[7] or Stephanie Siegel's *Parenting Your Adopted Child: A Complete and Loving Guide*.[8] These book will have much relevance in the years to come. For now, use them to understand some of the concerns you may face.

Previously mentioned adoption organizations or adoptive parents support groups are also invaluable resources (see Appendix I for contact information). They could, for example, provide you with the names of adoptive parents willing to share their experiences or the names of professionals in your area that members have found helpful. Continue to learn until you are confident that adoption is either not for you or an experience you will spend your whole life learning about.

One final thought: although you must acknowledge such differences, do not let them overwhelm you. The experience of anticipating possible problems can, if you let it, take away some of the excitement and joy at the possibility of parenting.

Once you have made the decision, once you have that child in your arms, nothing else will matter. Would you feel different about the child if the child had entered your family by birth? People who have children both by birth and by adoption say they feel no difference. I wonder if that is true.

I will never take the existence of my child for granted. Almost every day, I look at him with awe. I wonder if a biological parent feels that awe, expressed below, as passionately?

> I would not change anything that led me here. Because, you see, he is my son. It is so much more than the simple idea that I could not love a child any more than I love him. No one else could be my son. I am glad I cannot have a biological child, glad the public adoption agency was unhelpful, glad . . . [a previous adoption attempt failed]. If any of those events had not happened, my son would not be my son. Unimaginable.

These feelings are not unique. Every adoptive parent I know feels the same way.

Endnotes

[1] Johnston, Patricia Irwin. *Taking Charge of Infertility*. Indianapolis: Perspectives Press, 1994.

[2] _____. *Adopting after Infertility*. Indianapolis: Perspectives Press, 1992.

[3] Salzer, Linda. *Surviving Infertility: A Compassionate Guide through the Emotional Crisis of Infertility*. New York: HarperCollins Publishers, 1986, 1991.

[4] *Adoption in Canada*. Final Report. May 1993. Funded by National Welfare Grants, Health & Welfare Canada.

[5] *Becoming Adoptive Parents: Shifts in Identity from Biological Parenthood to Adoptive Parenthood Among Infertile Couples*. Ottawa: National Library of Canada, 1988. [6 microfiche] Thesis PhD. McMaster University, 1987.

[6] Melina, Lois. *Raising Adopted Children: A Manual for Adoptive Parents*. New York: Harper & Row, 1986.

[7] Schaffer, Judith and Christina Lindstrom. *How to Raise an Adopted Child*. New York: Crown, 1989.

[8] Siegel, Stephanie. *Parenting Your Adopted Child: A Complete and Loving Guide*. New York: Prentice Hall Press, 1989.

chapter · · · · · · · · · · · · · · · · · *2*

Getting Started

Less than thirty years ago, there was no need to talk about an *adoption world*. You would certainly not be reading a book on the adoption process.

Once you had decided that you wanted to consider adoption, you simply would have made an enquiring telephone call to a local government office. Adopting a newborn was a relatively quick and easy process. The number of newborns waiting for adoption far exceeded the number of people wanting to adopt.

Today, the situation is vastly different. With increased acceptance of single parenting and increased availability of abortion, placing a child for adoption is no longer the only answer to an unwanted pregnancy. In fact, it is the least-used response.

According to the 1993 National Adoption Study, the average wait to adopt a healthy newborn through the government is almost six years.[1] My discussions with the provincial governments revealed that even a six-year wait is optimistic—devastating news for anyone thinking of adoption as the way to create their family.

So you must enter the adoption world. You must learn about the other options available to you. You must take control of your life by actively working to create your family.

Taking Control

This book focuses on the adoption of a newborn through a Canadian *independent* or *identified adoption*, two types of *private adoption* that you will soon learn more about. These types of adoption are not the right choices for everyone. They make demands on your time and energy. They require you to give up your privacy. You must consider the needs of the people that scare you most—the biological parents or, as they are often called, the *birth parents* of your child.

Yet, in return, they allow you to do more than just sit and wait. You may search for a pregnant woman considering adoption for her unborn child. You may ask her to consider you as the adoptive parents of her child. The harder you work at letting people know you are looking, the greater your chances of success. Amazing—a process that allows you to regain some control over your life.

The idea that birth and adoptive parents choose each other may initially sound strange. However, it makes perfect sense; it is their lives that are affected by the decision. Why shouldn't the adoption professionals advise rather than decide? Even the government has acknowledged this argument. Nowadays, many adoptions arranged by the government—*public adoptions*—allow birth parents to choose the adoptive parents from preselected anonymous profiles.

Before you attempt to exercise this new-found control, you must learn. You must become an informed prospective adoptive parent. You must understand not only private adoption but all of your options—the complete adoption world. Only then will you be ready to make your adoption attack plan. A plan that will take into account what you want and what you practically and legally can do.

Whenever I learn about something new, there is a period of time when I am very uneasy. I feel ignorant, more ignorant than when I began. It seems that just as I start to acquire a little knowledge, it becomes clear that there is so much more to learn. I feel overwhelmed. I sometimes even panic.

Learning about adoption, and in particular, private adoption, is no different. In fact, I think it is worse. We start with misconceptions. The stakes are so high. How could the learning process be anything but difficult?

So be patient with yourself. Do not expect to grasp everything at once. Slowly work your way through the information provided. Stop when necessary. Persevere. Keep in mind that you can be successful; you can become a parent.

Before starting at the beginning with a general description of adoption in Canada, two discussions may be helpful. First, an attempt at addressing some of your fears about private adoption. Then, an introduction to your best sources of information.

Fears about Private Adoption

In the last few years, private adoption has been in the headlines fairly often. Unfortunately, most of the stories are sensational accounts of the very small number of private adoptions that have problems.

Everything you have heard about private adoption may make the process seem scary. "It is an illegal and unethical way to create your family . . . There are no healthy babies to adopt . . . You will wait forever . . . You need to have a relationship with the birth parents of your child . . . The birth parents will change their minds and reclaim the child . . . It will cost you a fortune. . . ."

Do not believe everything you hear. Some statements are true. Some are exaggerated. Some are simply wrong.

A Legal and Ethical Process

A private adoption is not complete until an adoption order has been granted by a court. The order will not be granted unless the adoption has been conducted according to the relevant laws.

What laws are relevant? In Canada, the relevant laws are those of the province in which the adoptive parents live and the province where the adopted child is born or lives. It is those laws that determine every step that may be taken. Laws that attempt to protect all of the parties involved: the child, the birth parents and the adoptive parents. Laws that determine details such as the methods prospective adoptive parents can use to search for their child, what fees and expenses may be paid by the adoptive parents, who must consent to the adoption, when those consents may be obtained, etc.

So, a "private" adoption does not mean an "illegal" adoption. It also does not mean an "unethical" adoption. Some people wrongly associate a private adoption with the buying and selling of a baby. No province allows payments to be made to birth parents to place their child for adoption. Therefore, no private adoption legally completed in Canada may involve such a practice.

The Wait

This book is all about *not* waiting forever to adopt a so-called "healthy newborn". According to the 1993 National Adoption Study, the average waiting time for a private adoption, using a paid adoption professional, is between twenty and twenty-one months.[2]

Those who search for their child rather than sit on a private waiting list, adopt even faster. My son was born, and in my arms, nine months after my husband and I started looking for him.

How were we able to adopt so fast? There is no question that we were lucky. But we helped make our luck. We worked hard to find our child. We took control.

A Relationship with the Birth Parents of Your Child

Your child will have birth parents. A simple fact. Yet perhaps the most difficult adoption concept for prospective adoptive parents to accept.

The idea that your child will have other parents, however you qualify the term, may initially make you feel ill. Suggesting you might want to meet them or have ongoing communication probably seems intolerable. You don't want to have anything to do with them. You don't even want to think about them; never mind have any kind of relationship with them. You simply want them to go away.

However, no matter how you adopt, what you know about them and them about you, they will continue to exist. Not only will they exist, but the biological connection they share with your child will ensure that their lives and your family's lives are forever linked. They are not going to go away.

At a minimum, that connection will cause mutual fantasizing at various times throughout your lives. You play an important part in who your child will be, but so do they; they provided the raw material. How can you and your child not wonder who they are, what they are like, what they look like, where they are, are they thinking about us, why did they agree to the adoption. . . .

Whether the birth parents of your child are more involved in your family's lives does depend on how you adopt, as well as what they and your family want. Some adoption methods allow only a minimum amount of involvement, while others permit or require more. Some birth parents and adoptive parents want no involvement, while others want more. Eventually your child may also want a say in the decision.

Before you jump up and say "no way am I going to have anything to do with my child's birth parents; show me the method that allows no involvement," make sure any decision is based on facts—and not fear.

The type of involvement being discussed is generally called *openness*, since it involves opening the lines of communication between the birth parents, the adoptive parents and the adoptee. Openness has several forms. It could mean some type of anonymous communication, a letter or personal meeting, arranged through an adoption professional. Or it could mean exchanging identifying information and dealing with each other directly. Communication could be one time only or continuous.

Most prospective adoptive parents initially recoil from these ideas. Many are only willing to listen because they realize their chances of adopting a newborn are greatly increased by being flexible. However, they often come to realize that a certain amount of openness is not only acceptable but often desirable for themselves and their children.

Openness does not mean sharing the parenting of your child. It means recognizing that there are other people who care about your child. It means putting yourself through some discomfort to achieve, at minimum, respect for those other people and possibly, a relationship that will benefit them as well as you and, more important, your child.

Part of you will always want your child's birth parents to disappear—the selfish "I don't want to share him" part. The rest of you will slowly begin to understand that they need not be threats to your relationship with your child.

Unlike previous generations, today's adopted children generally grow up knowing they are adopted. Their identity, and their relationship with their adoptive parents, are not suddenly thrown into turmoil by finding out a hidden secret. They understand that they and their adoptive parents are a self-contained family, but that they also have birth parents.

When my husband and I started discussing adoption, I was adamant that we would have nothing to do with the birth parents of our child. Threatened does not begin to describe how I felt. An open relationship might happen in that liberal enclave to the south, California, but not here, not with me.

Well, by the time we talked to the birth mother of our son, six months after we began searching, I had changed my mind. I was not only willing to meet her; I wanted to meet her. I was terrified, but I had come to realize that it would relieve her concerns about us and our concerns about her.

I wanted to be able to tell my child about her, to assure my child that she cared. I also wanted her to get to know us, to see how much love we had to give. This would, I hoped, make it easier for her to walk out of the hospital alone.

I was right. The meeting was wonderful. It created a trust that continues to this day.

Everyone goes through a period of confusion. Give yourself time to get used to these ideas. Do not let the possibility of a meeting or even a relationship with the birth parents of your child frighten you off just yet. Keep an open mind as the issue is explored in greater detail in the coming chapters. You may be surprised at how quickly the intolerable feels right. I was.

The Birth Parents Changing Their Minds

It does happen. Birth parents do change their minds and decide to parent their child. However, many prospective adoptive parents have images of a knock on the door years after the adoption and their child being wrested from them. This does not happen.

Most of the time, birth parents who change their minds, do so before the child has been placed with the adoptive parents. In addition, birth parents do not have the right to change their minds whenever they want.

Let's back up. The following will give you a general understanding of when birth parents can change their minds in a Canadian adoption. Birth parents must sign a consent to adoption. The consent cannot be signed until a set time after the baby is born. The birth parents are then allowed a set time to withdraw their consent, to change their minds. The amount of time until the consent can be signed and the amount of time the consent can be withdrawn varies depending on the provinces involved. Once those time periods have run out, the birth parents cannot change their minds.

Generally, the hardest times for the birth parents are just before and just after the birth. Therefore, if the adoption plan is going to fall apart, it usually happens before the birth parents sign the consent to adoption and before the adoptive parents have the child in their home.

We will discuss ways to help minimize the risk. We will also discuss ways to help deal with the stress the risk causes. There is not, however, an easy way to eliminate the risk.

You should realize that, generally, the same risk exists in all Canadian adoptions of newborns. The consent procedures of most provinces are the same whether the adoption is private or public.

It might help you to know that my husband and I survived a birth mother changing her mind. At the time, it was very painful. Yet, we look back now and realize that it was just one more step on the way to finding our son. Hindsight always makes things look easier. But you too will be able to look back on any pain as part of a long labour.

The Cost

The cost of a private adoption varies. However, there are a few points that can help give you an idea of how much you would need to spend. First, as previously mentioned, it is illegal in Canada for birth parents to receive any payment in connection with the adoption of their child. You cannot pay them, directly or indirectly, a fee.

Your primary costs will be for services from various adoption professionals. Generally, you may legally only pay for certain types of services such as counselling for yourself and the birth parents, gathering background information from the birth parents, and providing the legal and administrative assistance required in completing the adoption. According to the 1993 National Adoption Study, the average cost of these primary services varies between $4,528 and $5,873.[3]

Secondary costs stem from the actual search for the birth parents of your child and, therefore, your child. Certain methods, such as advertising and sending out mailings, will increase your costs. The costs of other methods, such as networking, are negligible.

The higher fees you sometimes hear about generally occur in an *international adoption* or a U.S. private adoption, two alternatives to a Canadian private adoption that will be discussed in Chapter 5. An international adoption, where the child to be adopted is born outside of Canada, obviously requires additional spending. For example, there are the foreign-country administrative and legal costs and, often, the costs of travelling to and having an extended stay in that country.

A U.S. private adoption is generally more expensive than its Canadian counterpart because many U.S. birth mothers do not have any health insurance. The birth mother's medical expenses during the pregnancy, and sometimes living expenses, are often paid for by the adoptive parents.

* * *

There are other statements about the adoption process that will probably scare you. If something concerns you, keep it in mind as you continue to learn. Allow yourself time to understand the complete picture.

You have probably gone through much anguish to get to this point. The adoption process may initially increase your suffering. The infertility treatments, while painful and frustrating, are no longer scary; you know what to expect. The adoption process is an unknown. Once again you will feel out of control. However, it should not be long before a new emotion surfaces: *hope.*

Adoption Resources

This book represents the start of your adoption learning process. It may be all you need. More likely, you will want additional help and support throughout your adoption experience. The rest of this chapter will introduce the types of resources available.

During various discussions throughout the book, specific resources will be suggested. Use those resources, whenever you feel that the topic of discussion needs further examination.

Government Adoption Authorities

The province where you live has a department or ministry responsible for adoptions. Contact information is listed in Chapter 4. The department can answer questions about the adoption process in your province. It is not, however, your best resource.

Adoptive Parents

Your best sources of information and support for anything to do with adoption, from should I adopt to how do I adopt to how do I parent, are those who have already adopted. They alone know exactly what you are going through. Every emotion you are feeling, every issue that concerns you has been experienced by them.

You may already know adoptive parents, or a friend may have friends who are adoptive parents. Do not hesitate to ask if they will talk to you. You may initially feel shy about asking someone to talk about something that seems so private, but most adoptive parents are glad to help. Any need for privacy with respect to creating their family was likely forgotten a long time ago. As well, someone else probably helped them get started, so they are happy to pass on the favour.

Listen to their story. Not only should it encourage you, it should help you focus on what you must do and where you have concerns. Tell them those concerns, ask for their advice. Also ask for the names of adoption resources in your community that they found helpful.

Adoptive Parent Support Groups

If you do not know anyone who has adopted, or even if you do, consider joining a local adoptive parent support group. Many of these groups include both prospective adoptive and adoptive parents. Besides aiding the informal sharing of experiences, concerns and information, many groups have formal educational sessions that focus on a variety of topics of interest.

Just as important as the knowledge you will gain are the friends you and, later, your child will make through meetings and social events. These friends can do something that most other friends cannot—know when and how to encourage you and when to let you cry.

Besides regional support groups, there are groups that have a more specific focus; a focus that may interest you. For example, there are groups for single adoptive parents, groups for special needs adoptive parents, and groups for families formed by international adoption.

Appendix I lists adoptive parent support groups. Find a group that is close by or of interest and give them a call. If there is a meeting scheduled, attend and learn. If there is no meeting in the near future, ask if there are members willing to talk to you about their experiences.

Adoption Organizations

In addition to local- and specific-focus adoptive parent groups, there are adoption groups or organizations that have a broader focus. There are two Canada-wide organizations of interest—the Adoption Council of Canada and the Infertility Awareness Association of Canada—and several provincial organizations. These organizations, and some of the larger adoptive parent support groups, generally help their adoption community by performing services such as:

- maintaining a telephone information and referral line
- operating a resource library
- publishing a newsletter
- advocating for their community with the government
- helping co-ordinate educational programs
- assisting the formation of local support groups.

Appendix I also lists these organizations. Join your provincial and/or a Canadian organization. While many of their services are available to the public, membership includes receipt of their newsletters and mailings—an important link to your adoption community.

The National Adoption Information Clearinghouse (NAIC) is a good source of information. NAIC was established by the U.S. Congress to provide easy access to information on all aspects of adoption. The services of NAIC that may be of interest to Canadians include:

- searching an adoption literature data base and supplying a series of abstracts and bibliographic information on a particular adoption topic

- providing referrals to experts knowledgeable in various areas of adoption practice
- publishing a variety of factsheets on adoption issues
- making available U.S. government reports on adoption
- supplying excerpts of state and federal adoption laws.

Many of NAIC services are free to residents of the U.S. Depending on the service requested, there may be a charge for Canadians. Contact NAIC to request a catalogue of its publications and services (see Appendix I).

Adoption Newsletters and Magazines

Some of the support groups and organizations produce newsletters or magazines. There are also a number of free-standing adoption publications. All of these publications are invaluable sources of information.

The adoption world is constantly changing. There is always something new—new laws, new policies, new sources of adoptable children, new adoption professionals, new resources, new concerns, new ideas. Adoption newsletters and magazines are the only way to keep abreast of these changes.

Many communities have events that are of interest to prospective adoptive and adoptive parents—informational seminars, speakers, support group meetings and even local television and radio programming. Events that you will not be aware of unless you are plugged into the local adoption community.

Appendix II lists Canadian and American newsletters and magazines. Subscribe to at least one of the newsletters in your province or the *Newsletter Bulletin* of the Adoption Council of Canada (ACC) to keep abreast of provincial news. The Toronto newsletter, *Adoption Helper*, edited by Katherin Jones and published by Robin R. Hilborn, is also a terrific source for both prospective adoptive and adoptive parents living anywhere in Canada, especially with respect to international adoption.

American publications, while not generally helpful with respect to the Canadian adoption process, are often good sources of articles on general adoption topics. One of the best is the magazine *Adoptive Families* (formerly *Ours*), produced by the largest adoptive parent organization in the U.S., Adoptive Families of America. It has a circulation of 15,000 and combines articles on topics of interest with the latest in adoption news.

There are also a large number of American specific-focus newsletters and magazines. For example, there are publications for single parents, Jewish families, parents of special-needs children, multi-racial families and for parents of children born in Romania, India, Chile, Peru, Haiti, Germany and Guatemala; there are even publications for those who want to focus on feminist views or fight racism in adoption.

Books and Audiotapes

There are many books and audio cassettes about adoption. Unfortunately, almost all of them are geared towards an American audience. While this is not a problem when dealing with issues such as infertility or parenting an adopted child, it is a problem with respect to the adoption process. As mentioned earlier, the adoption process varies depending on where the adoptive parents and the child to be adopted live. The only other book which deals specifically with the Canadian adoption process is John Bowen's helpful book *A Canadian Guide to International Adoptions.*[4]

Appendix III contains a list of the books I found helpful and interesting. There are many other good books, and a more complete list can be obtained from *Adoption Helper* or from William Lewis Gage (contact information in Appendix III).

Finding the books you want is not always easy. If you cannot locate them in your neighbourhood bookstore or public library, see if your provincial adoption organization has a resource library or look for a bookstore that specializes in parenting issues. If you still cannot find the books you want, you may need to obtain the books by mail—a second best alternative since you cannot glance through the books to determine if they are what you need. Some organizations will send you a catalogue describing the adoption and infertility resources they sell; for example, the Adoptive Families of America (AFA) and Tapestry books.. You could also contact a publisher of a particular book directly.

If you prefer listening to audio cassettes, there are several to choose from. The Infertility Association of Canada (IAAC) tapes the seminars they conduct on various infertility and adoption topics. Contact IAAC for a listing of these tapes. Lois Melina and Patricia Irwin Johnston, two respected authors, have each recorded several tapes on various adoption topics. A listing of Melina's tapes, as well as her books and newsletter, can be requested from the Adopted Child Library. A listing of Johnston's tapes, as well as infertility and adoption books written by her and others, can be requested from Perspectives Press. AFA's catalogue of adoption resources also contains numerous tapes.

Contact information for the adoption organizations discussed above

(ACC, the provincial adoption organizations, AFA and IAAC) is listed in Appendix I. Contact information for the Adopted Child Library is found in Appendix II. A catalogue may be obtained from Tapestry Books at 908-806-6695 and from Perspectives Press at 317-872-3055.

Studies

There have been several recent Canadian studies focusing on adoption. Depending on your interests, you may wish to examine one or more of them:

- Kerry J. Daly and Michael P. Sobol's *Adoption in Canada* is the 1993 National Adoption Study which examines key adoption trends, reviews existing policy and legislation, explores the factors associated with pregnancy decision making and surveys the provision of adoption services in Canada.
- Anne Westhues and Joyce S. Cohen's *Intercountry Adoption in Canada*[5] examines how internationally adopted children and their families fare when the child has reached adolescence.
- Nancy J. Cohen, James Duvall and James C. Coyne's *Mental Health Service Needs of Post-Adoptive Families.*[6]

Adoption Professionals

There are a number of different individuals and groups that assist prospective adoptive parents. Who these professionals are and what they do is often confusing, since the type of professional does not always signify the type of service. A lawyer may do more than advise you on the law; a social worker may do more than counsel. For this reason, this book uses the term *adoption professional* to designate a person who performs the service being discussed unless a particular profession generally performs that service.

Some of these professionals have government funding, while others are funded through charitable donations. Most charge fees for their services.

How to find and use these professionals will be explained in the next few chapters. For now, understand that there are basically three different services that may be provided to prospective adoptive parents: assistance in finding their child, counselling for themselves and the birth parents of their child, and legal assistance in completing the adoption. An adoption professional may provide any number of these services.

Also keep in mind that your province determines who can be paid for what type of service. Do not make any payments before making sure that they are permitted by law. The legal completion of your child's adoption may be at stake.

Endnotes

[1] Average waiting time of 5 years, 11 months, with 25 percent of public agencies reporting waiting times of 8 to 12 years. *Adoption in Canada*, 52.

[2] *Adoption in Canada*, 52.

[3] *Adoption in Canada*, 54.

[4] Bowen, John. *A Canadian Guide to International Adoptions.* North Vancouver: Self-Counsel Press, 1992.

[5] Westhues, Anne, and Joyce S. Cohen. *Intercountry Adoption in Canada.* Final Report. January 1994. Funded by National Welfare Grants, Human Resources Development Canada.

[6] Cohen, Nancy J., and James Duvall and James C. Coyne. *Mental Health Service Needs of Post-Adoptive Families.* Final Report. January 1994. Funded by National Welfare Grants, Health & Welfare Canada.

chapter • • • • • • • • • • • • • • • 3

Understanding Adoption in Canada

In 1981, almost 78 percent of Canadian newborn adoptees were adopted publicly. Since 1988, more Canadian newborns have been adopted privately than publicly.[1] What exactly is a public adoption? What is a private adoption? Why has there been such a dramatic shift from one to the other?

Public Adoptions

A *public* or *government adoption* is an adoption arranged or funded by a government body. A Canadian public adoption is arranged or funded by one of the provincial governments.

Each province has a government department or ministry whose responsibilities include adoptions. Public adoptions are processed by branches of that government department or by agencies, societies or other organizations funded by that government department. These *public agencies* work with the prospective birth and adoptive parents in their community.

The Process

A public agency must follow its provincial laws and procedures. While there are differences between the provinces, generally those hoping to publicly adopt a Canadian newborn have a similar experience.

First, they contact the public agency handling adoptions in the area they live. Then they wait. They are sent an application form to complete and return. Then they wait. They may be invited to attend information or orientation sessions. Then they wait. Eventually they participate in an assessment and preparation process, often called a *homestudy*, and complete any other government requirements. Then they wait.

The total waiting time depends on the number of prospective birth and adoptive parents working with that public agency. In several provinces, this wait cannot be measured since there are so few newborns without *special needs* (discussed below) available for adoption. The average estimated wait for the other provinces is almost eight years.[2]

Some public agencies have their employees match birth and adoptive parents. Others allow birth parents to choose the adoptive parents of their birth child from a selection of anonymous profiles. The profiles presented to the birth parents often represent those prospective adoptive parents who have been waiting the longest and have particular characteristics requested by the birth parents.

After the birth, the birth parents consent to the adoption and the public agency places the child with the chosen adoptive parents. Generally, the placement is directly from the hospital, but sometimes a temporary foster home takes care of the child until the consents have been signed or until the consents can no longer be withdrawn.

The next few months are considered a probationary period. During this time, a social worker will visit the prospective adoptive parents' home to help with any problems and do a post-placement assessment. If everything is going smoothly, an application for an adoption order is submitted to the courts at the end of the period.

Once the court issues the order, the adoption is complete. The birth and adoption records are sealed; a birth certificate using the adoptive parents' family name is issued. The adoptive parents are now the legal parents of the child, as if the child was born to them.

The public agency is also responsible for providing counselling to the adoptive and birth parents, gathering background information on the birth parents and otherwise ensuring that all legal and administrative details of the adoption are completed. All of this is done at no or nominal cost (ignoring taxes) to the parties.

The Focus

Public agencies do not focus on the needs of prospective adoptive parents. Their mandate is to find families for the children in their care.

Children enter the care of a public agency when their birth parents can no longer provide for them. Sometimes the children are voluntarily surrendered by their birth parents. Often they come into care by way of the courts because they have been abused or neglected.

Most children in the care of public agencies have *special needs*. Therefore, the majority of public adoptions are also *special-needs adoptions*. Generally, children are considered to have special needs if they are physically, emotionally or cognitively challenged; older; part of a sibling group; of racial or ethnic minority status; or have a history that suggests future problems.

A special-needs adoption may be very different from the adoption experience described above. This type of adoption is discussed further in Chapter 5.

Private Adoptions

The meaning of the term *private adoption* is not uniform. In Canada, it generally means any adoption that is not a public adoption; that is, not arranged by a public agency.

There are three different types of Canadian private adoptions. Two types have already been mentioned as the focus of this book, *independent adoption* and *identified adoption*. We will call the third type a *licensee adoption*.

All three types of private adoption are not available to every prospective adoptive parent. Each province has enacted laws that specify which type of private adoption it requires or permits and what procedures must be taken to complete the adoption.

The following discussion is intended to give you a general understanding of these types of adoption. What you can and cannot do in your province is discussed in the next chapter. It is, however, important for you to see the overall picture. Such an understanding will give you a better sense of the restrictions you face in your province and whether it makes sense to venture outside your province.

Licensee Adoptions

A licensee adoption is processed by, surprise, a *licensee*. A licensee is an adoption professional, either an agency or an individual, that has met the licensing requirements of its provincial government. Licensed agencies are often staffed by social workers with a lawyer available to do any necessary legal work. Licensed individuals are generally lawyers, social workers or doctors. Licensee adoptions currently exist in four provinces: Alberta, Ontario, Prince Edward Island and Saskatchewan.

The Process

Generally, when the licensee is an agency, the adoption experience is very similar to a public adoption. If you ignore the wait and cost discussions, you could reread the above public adoption process section, replacing "public agency" with "licensed agency."

Like a public agency, a licensed agency generally provides a full-service adoption. Both prospective birth and adoptive parents are helped. Pregnant women considering adoption are counselled on all of their alternatives. If and when they are ready to proceed with an adoption, the necessary steps are taken.

Prospective adoptive parents simply follow the instructions of the licensed agency until they become adoptive parents. They fill out an application form and are placed on a waiting list. As they move up the list, the licensed agency provides the needed counselling and assessment services. Eventually they are matched with a birth parent and the adoption is legally completed. The government approvals required before placement are obtained. The consents to the adoption are signed. The probation period is survived. The adoption order is issued.

Some licensed individuals provide prospective adoptive parents with the same services as an agency—matching the prospective adoptive parents with their child, counselling them and the birth parents of their child and legal completion of the adoption. Other licensed individuals are only involved in providing counselling or legal services. They or the prospective adoptive parents must arrange to complete any component they do not provide. More about this type of adoption, an identified adoption, below.

The Differences

Although the process is similar to that of a public adoption, there are advantages to a licensee adoption. First, birth parents avoid working with the same public agency that is responsible for taking children away from abusive parents—a public agency that is seen, sometimes unfairly, as uncaring of the birth parents' concerns since its primary interest is always that of the child.

Similarly, since a licensee does not have children in its care, its focus is on finding children for families rather than finding families for children. These facts do not mean that the concerns of the child are forgotten, but that resources can be spent on ensuring that the concerns of the adoptive and birth parents are also addressed.

With a licensee adoption, both the prospective birth and adoptive parents may choose with whom they wish to work. They need not go to their local public agency, but may pick the licensee that best meets their needs.

A licensee is often more flexible than a public agency in deciding the openness of an adoption. Birth parents are allowed more say in who will be the adoptive parents of their birth child and the type of relationship they will have with the adoptive family.

Although public agencies are slowly adding more openness to their procedures, they generally lag behind the private adoption world. Their procedures are often formally entrenched, preventing a quick response to the wishes of their clients.

Public agencies sometimes specify a maximum age for adoptive parents or require the adoptive parents to be childless. Licensees rarely have such restrictions.

These advantages contribute to the major reason prospective adoptive parents choose licensee adoptions over public adoptions. Birth parents generally prefer licensee adoptions to public adoptions. This results in more newborns being available for adoption through a licensee. Therefore, the adoption of a newborn who does not have special needs is usually faster through a licensee than through a public agency.

The major disadvantage of a licensee adoption is the cost. Unlike with a public adoption, the adoptive parents generally pay for any services provided by the licensee. As previously mentioned, according to the 1993 National Adoption Study, the average cost of private adoption services varies between $4,528 and $5,873.[3]

Independent Adoptions

In an *independent* or *direct adoption*, the prospective adoptive and birth parents control the process. There is no public agency or licensee involved. The birth parents have the legal right to place the child directly into the adoptive parents' home. Independent adoptions are permitted in every province except Ontario, P.E.I. and Quebec.

The Process

The majority of this book is devoted to helping you understand the independent adoption process. Unlike a public or licensee adoption, an independent adoption is usually a *self-directed adoption* rather than a full-service adoption. One does not simply join a waiting list and follow instructions. Prospective adoptive parents attempting an independent adoption must take the initiative. Therefore, they need help in understanding exactly what they can and must do.

Generally, an independent adoption requires the prospective adoptive parents to find their child by searching for a pregnant woman considering adoption for her unborn child. Adoption professionals are hired to counsel and legally complete the adoption.

Some provinces have a few unlicensed agencies that will provide full-service independent adoptions. However, care must be taken when dealing with such agencies. First, most provinces regulate who can be paid for what type of service. Make sure it is legal to pay the unlicensed agency for the services they intend to provide. Second, there is no set procedures that these agencies must follow. Confirm that none of the required components of the adoption are missing. Do not hand over the reigns of your adoption without further investigation.

The Differences

An independent adoption is different from a public adoption in some of the same ways a licensee adoption is different. The prospective birth and adoptive parents avoid working with their local public agency and may instead choose the adoption professionals with whom they wish to work. There is no maximum age or number of children restriction. The adoptive parents generally pay for any services provided by the adoption professionals.

There are also several ways it is different from both public and licensee adoptions. Prospective adoptive parents may do more than join a waiting list and hope. They may take control of their lives by working hard at finding their child. They may speed up the process by adding their energy.

This is an advantage. Most of us would like to be able to adopt our child through a full-service adoption. We would like to make a phone call, be told what to do and when to pick up our child. Unfortunately, for many of us, this is not a timely reality. Being able to influence the waiting time is, therefore, an advantage. A scary advantage, but an advantage nevertheless. Making this advantage less scary and using it successfully is what this book is all about.

In an independent adoption, there is no third party (other than the law) stating what can and cannot be done. The prospective birth and adoptive parents make the important decisions—for example, concerning the match and the degree of openness in the adoption.

This also means there is no third party responsible for ensuring that the adoption is successfully completed. The prospective adoptive parents must take that responsibility, hiring experienced adoption professionals to help whenever possible.

Often, the legal requirements of an independent adoption are less vigorous. The adoptive parents may not need to complete a homestudy before the placement of a child in their home. The birth parents may not need to be counselled.

Fewer restrictions is usually an advantage. It can become a disadvantage if important steps in the adoption are forgotten—

specifically, counselling. Both the adoptive and birth parents must understand their options and be fully prepared for the adoption experience, if the experience is to be successful.

Independent adoptions completed in Manitoba or New Brunswick have a notable disadvantage over public adoptions completed in the province. These provinces allow the birth parents in an independent adoption to withdraw their consents up until the issuance of the adoption order. This is a long time, given that the application for the order cannot even be made before the child has lived with the prospective adoptive parents for six months.

The other provinces have either no time or a relatively short period of time in which the birth parents may simply withdraw their consents. In addition, these provinces do not generally differentiate between public and private adoptions with respect to the withdrawal right.

Identified Adoptions

The final type of adoption, an *identified* or *designated adoption*, is a hybrid. It combines features of independent and licensee adoptions. Identified adoptions exist in Ontario and Prince Edward Island.

The Process
Like an independent adoption, an identified adoption is self-directed. The prospective adoptive parents find their child themselves by searching for a pregnant woman considering adoption for her unborn child. The "identified" birth parents are then referred to a chosen licensee. The licensee is used to provide, or arrange for, the necessary counselling and the legal completion of the adoption.

The Differences
An identified adoption is perhaps the best of all worlds. It encompasses the most advantageous feature of each of the other two types of private adoption. Prospective adoptive parents may speed up the adoption process by working hard to find their child. There is a third party, the licensee, that is responsible for ensuring that the adoption is successfully completed.

As with all Canadian private adoptions, the prospective birth and adoptive parents avoid working with their local public agency and may instead choose the adoption professionals with whom they wish to work. Similarly, there is no maximum age or number of children restriction and the adoptive parents generally pay for any services provided by the adoption professionals.

Adopting a Child Born in Another Province

Most Canadians who privately adopt, do adopt a child born in the province where they live. However, it is possible to adopt a child born in a different province. I live in Ontario; my son was born in British Columbia.

Adopting a child born in a different province often adds complications and expense. Two sets of laws must be considered; travelling may be required. There are, however, circumstances when it is desirable.

Residents of Quebec have no choice; the private adoption of a child born in Quebec is not permitted. If they wish to privately adopt, they must find a child born outside of Quebec and complete the adoption by having the order issued or recognized in Quebec.

Residents of other provinces adopt a child born in a different province for various reasons. An opportunity may have presented itself by chance. They may have roots or connections in another province that makes searching in that province easier. They may feel that increasing the geographical boundaries of their search will increase their chances of success, or perhaps that the laws and procedures of another province are more advantageous than those of their own.

Not all provinces allow residents of other provinces to adopt a child born within the province. Those provinces that do allow non-residents to adopt, and whose rules must be followed, are discussed in the next chapter.

Making Sense of the Canadian Alternatives

Okay, let's make some sense of what you have just been told. There are several ways to adopt a Canadian newborn. You may pursue a public adoption. If you live in Alberta, Ontario, P.E.I. or Saskatchewan, you may complete a licensee adoption. Both options are usually full-service adoptions. You get on the waiting list of either the public agency or an agency or individual licensed by your province and follow their instructions. Generally, a licensee adoption is faster and more expensive than a public adoption.

In addition, or as an alternative, you may complete a self-directed adoption. You find your child yourself by locating a pregnant woman considering adoption for her unborn child. Depending on where you and the child to be adopted lives, you would work with either a licensee (an identified adoption) or other adoption professionals (an independent adoption) to complete the adoption. Generally, this is the fastest and most time and energy demanding alternative.

Residents of Quebec must search for their child outside of their province. Everyone else may search inside as well as outside their province.

The next chapter explains what you legally can and must do to complete an independent or identified adoption in each of the provinces. Part II of this book explains how to search for your child. Finally, what to do once you have found your child is the focus of Part III.

Endnotes

[1] *Adopting in Canada*, 9.
[2] The average estimated wait is based on discussions with provincial authorities. See the provincial summaries contained in Chapter 4 for each province's estimated wait.
[3] *Adopting in Canada*, 54.

chapter • • • • • • • • • • • • • • • • • 4

Demystifying the Legal Process

An adoption, whether private or public, is not legally complete until an adoption order has been issued. Once that adoption order is issued, a prospective adoptive parent becomes an adoptive parent or, even better, simply a parent. The legal goal of your adoption experience is, therefore, to do everything necessary and nothing forbidden in the quest for the adoption order.

Adoption is the responsibility of the provinces. Each province either has an adoption statute or controls the adoption process within a more general child welfare act. It is these laws, and any government practices that have developed, that you must follow.

The procedures required to complete a self-directed adoption— either an independent or an identified adoption— have been set out in a separate summary for each province. Each summary also contains some helpful general information about adoption in the province. At the end of the chapter, there is a discussion on adopting a child born in a province other than where you live. For now, review the summary for the province where you live. Looking at other provinces will be addressed when you make your adoption plan in Chapter 6.

Each provincial summary has four sections containing questions and answers. Although very specific procedures have been stipulated throughout the summaries, there may be some leeway. A judge generally has the freedom to do what is required to meet the *best interests of the child*. A date missed or a procedure mishandled is not necessarily a problem. However, horror stories do exist and there are no guarantees.

While the information in the summaries has been reviewed by representatives of the provincial departments responsible for adoptions, keep in mind that laws and procedures change and that the summaries cannot cover every possible situation. Do not rely solely on the summaries—seek the advice of an experienced adoption professional. Finding that adoption professional is addressed in Chapter 6.

Throughout each summary, there are several references to notes. Make sure you read the accompanying notes found at the end of the chapter at least once. They provide important information that applies to all of the provinces.

The discussion in each summary pertains to an adoption of a newborn not of Native descent. Neither prospective adoptive parent is a step-parent or otherwise related to the child or the birth parents of the child.

Do not let your provincial summary overwhelm you. At this stage in your learning process, use the information to obtain a general sense of the legal steps in your adoption. You can refer to the summary for specific information as required.

ALBERTA

Public Adoptions

What public agency processes public adoptions?
A district office of the Alberta Family and Social Services Department arranges public adoptions for members of its community.
Contact: Check local telephone book or call the Alberta Family and Social Services Department, Adoption Services listed below.

What is the estimated wait to adopt a newborn (who does not have special needs) through a public agency?[1]
Eight to nine years.

Private Adoptions—General

What types of private adoption are available?[2]

1. Licensee Adoptions: Yes, through a *Licensed Adoption Agency*.
2. Independent Adoptions: Yes, sometimes referred to as *direct placements*.
3. Identified Adoptions: No.

What adoption expenses and fees may prospective adoptive parents pay?[3]

1. Cannot give any payment or reward, whether direct or indirect, to (i) procure or assist in procuring, or (ii) to place or facilitate the placement of a child for purposes of an adoption in or outside Alberta.
2. Reasonable fees, expenses or disbursements may, however, be paid to (i) a qualified person in respect of the preparation of a homestudy or *home assessment,* (ii) a lawyer in respect of legal services, (iii) a physician in respect of medical services provided to the child to be adopted (the birth mother is expected to have or obtain medical coverage), and (iv) a Licensed Adoption Agency in respect of certain defined expenses.

What other general information about private adoption should prospective adoptive parents know?

1. Prospective adoptive parents may apply to a district office of the Alberta Family and Social Services Department to complete a public adoption and to one Licensed Adoption Agency to complete a licensee adoption. They may not work with more than one Licensed Adoption Agency at a time. This constraint does not affect the ability to do an independent adoption.
2. There are also unlicensed adoption agencies in Alberta. However, given the above list of payments that may be made in connection with an adoption, generally (i) only a lawyer or a Licensed Adoption Agency may act as a paid intermediary, and (ii) payments may not be for simply bringing the adoptive and birth parents together.

Independent Adoptions

A. The Search

Which of the search methods discussed in Part II of this book may prospective adoptive parents use to find their child themselves?

1. Networking: Yes.
2. Advertising: No.
3. Mailings: No. *(Alta. cont'd)*

B. The Consent

Who must consent to the adoption?[4]

1. The consent to adoption must be signed by each *Guardian* of the child to be adopted. The birth mother is always considered a Guardian. The birth father will generally be considered a Guardian if he (i) was married to the birth mother at the time of the birth of the child, (ii) was married to the birth mother of the child and the marriage was terminated not more than 300 days before the birth of the child, (iii) lived with the birth mother for at least one year immediately before the birth of the child, (iv) married the birth mother after the birth of the child and has acknowledged that he is the father of the child, or (v) has been granted guardianship by the court.
2. Birth parents who are under the age of majority may still consent to the adoption.

When and how may the consent be signed?

1. The consent may be signed any time after the birth of the child.
2. A representative of the Director of the Alberta Family and Social Services Department (the "Director") must witness the signing of the consent.
3. The consent signed by the Guardians is for a specific family identified in the consent. Therefore, the birth and adoptive parents of a child are aware of each other's full names.

When and how may the consent be withdrawn?
Not later than ten days after the signing, by written notice to the Director.

C. The Placement

What approvals and notifications are required before a child is placed in the prospective adoptive parents' home?

1. Before the placement, a home assessment report must be prepared if a private guardianship order is being sought (discussed below). Otherwise, no approvals or notifications are required.
2. If the birth mother gives her permission, the child may be placed with the prospective adoptive parents directly from the hospital before the consent to adoption is signed.

What is required immediately after the placement?

1. Within 30 days of the placement, the prospective adoptive parents and the birth parents must notify the Director of the placement.[7]
2. Upon receiving notification of the placement, the Director will instigate an investigation. This investigation is conducted by a social worker and includes a review of the circumstances of the match, a home assessment (even if one was conducted to obtain a private guardianship order), child welfare record and criminal record checks and obtaining reference letters and medical examinations.
3. At the time of writing, social workers conducting investigations were employed by Alberta Family and Social Services. However, it is anticipated that social workers employed by Licensed Adoption Agencies will soon take over this function.

What other placement information should prospective adoptive parents know?

Generally, the prospective adoptive parents obtain a private guardianship order. Otherwise, the birth parents remain the guardians of the child until the adoption order is issued.[8]

D. The Adoption Order

When and how is the adoption order obtained?

1. An adoption order is issued by a judge of the Court of Queen's Bench after a successful hearing. The Director requests a hearing on behalf of the prospective adoptive parents by filing a petition for an adoption order with the court.[9]
2. A petition for an order may be filed anytime after the ten-day period for withdrawal of the consent has elapsed. However, the petition cannot be made until the supporting material (investigation reports, certificate of live birth, etc.) is available.
3. Thirty days before the date fixed for the hearing of the petition, the prospective adoptive parents must give the Guardians of the child and the birth father of the child, whether or not he is a Guardian, notice of the hearing date and a copy of the petition.

(Alta. cont'd)

When is the order generally issued?
Ten to twelve months after placement.

Government Contact

Which government department or ministry is responsible for adoptions?
The Alberta Family and Social Services Department. Contact:
Alberta Family and Social Services
Adoption Services
9th Floor, Seventh Street Plaza
10030 – 107th Street
Edmonton, Alberta T5J 3E4
Tel: (403) 422-0177
Fax: (403) 427-2048

How does this government department help individual prospective adoptive parents?

1. Answers general questions about either private or public adoption. However, a local public agency may be more helpful with respect to procedural questions and should therefore be contacted first.
2. Produces a brochure entitled *Adoptions in Alberta* and a list of Licensed Adoption Agencies that are distributed by the local public agencies.

BRITISH COLUMBIA

Public Adoptions

What public agency processes public adoptions?
A district office of the Ministry of Social Services arranges public adoptions for members of its community.
Contact: Check local telephone book or call the Ministry of Social Services, Adoption Section, listed below.

What is the estimated wait to adopt a newborn (who does not have special needs) through a public agency?[1]
Five to six years.

Private Adoptions—General

What types of private adoption are available?[2]

1. Licensee Adoptions: No.
2. Independent Adoptions: Yes.
3. Identified Adoptions: No.

What adoption expenses and fees may prospective adoptive parents pay?[3]

1. Cannot offer money or consideration of any kind to (i) induce a person to make a child available for adoption or (ii) in respect of procuring or assisting in procuring a child for adoption.
2. There is no stipulation of the type of payments which may be made by prospective adoptive parents. Paying expenses of the birth parents may be "offering consideration of any kind" and should only be done with the written permission of the Superintendent of Family and Child Service (the "Superintendent").

What other general information about private adoption should prospective adoptive parents know?

1. There are unlicensed agencies that can provide full-service adoptions to prospective adoptive parents. The Adoptive Parents Association of British Columbia (contact information in Appendix I) can provide information about such agencies.
2. Private adoption procedures are currently being reviewed by the government. There will probably be changes to the legislation in the next few years. It is unclear what form those changes will take.

Independent Adoptions

A. The Search

Which of the search methods discussed in Part II of this book may prospective adoptive parents use to find their child themselves?

1. Networking: Yes.
2. Advertising: No.
3. Mailings: Yes.

(B.C. cont'd)

B. The Consent

Who must consent to the adoption?[4]

1. The consent to adoption must be signed by each *Parent* of the child to be adopted. The birth mother is always considered a Parent. The birth father will generally be considered a Parent if he (i) signs the child's Registration of Live Birth, (ii) is or was the guardian of the child, (iii) acknowledges paternity of the child and has either custody or access rights, or (iv) acknowledges paternity of the child and has supported, maintained or cared for the child.
2. The court has the discretion to accept the consent of birth parents who are under the age of majority without the intervention of the guardians of the birth parents. Generally, a minor's consent is accepted.

When and how may the consent be signed?

1. The consent may not be signed by the birth mother until the child is a full ten days old. There is no similar restriction for the birth father; although, he cannot sign the consent before the birth of the child.
2. Generally, the signing of the consent is witnessed by a lawyer who is not representing the prospective adoptive parents. The persons signing the consent and the witness must sign affidavits stating that the effect of the consent and of the adoption was fully explained and that the consent was signed freely and voluntarily.[5]

When and how may the consent be withdrawn?

Cannot be withdrawn or *revoked* unless it is shown to the court's satisfaction that it is in the best interests of the child.[6]

C. The Placement

What approvals and notifications are required before a child is placed in the prospective adoptive parents' home?

1. No government approvals or notifications are required.
2. If the birth mother gives written permission, the child may be placed with the prospective adoptive parents directly from the hospital before the consent to adoption is signed. The exact

procedure varies depending on the hospital. Sometimes the birth mother must leave the hospital with the child and then hand the child to the prospective adoptive parents' lawyer.

What is required immediately after the placement?
Within fourteen days of the placement, the prospective adoptive parents and anyone who placed or facilitated the placement of the child must notify the Superintendent. The person who places or facilitates the placement of the adoption must complete a report which includes an explanation of the circumstances of the placement.[7]

What other placement information should prospective adoptive parents know?
The birth parents remain the guardians of the child until the adoption order is issued.[8]

D. The Adoption Order

When and how is the adoption order obtained?

1. An adoption order is issued by a judge of the Supreme Court of British Columbia after a successful hearing. The prospective adoptive parents request a hearing by filing an application for an adoption order with the court.[9]
2. Six months before filing an application, the prospective adoptive parents must notify the Superintendent of their intention to file the application.
3. Upon receiving the notification, the Superintendent will instigate an inquiry of the placement. This inquiry is conducted by a social worker employed by the Ministry of Social Services and includes a review of the circumstances of the placement and a homestudy which includes medical reports, criminal record checks and prior contact with the Ministry checks.
4. Twenty-one days before the date fixed for the hearing of the application, the prospective adoptive parents must give the Superintendent notice of the hearing date and a copy of the application.
5. Before the hearing, the Superintendent will file with the court a report of the inquiry of the placement with a recommendation to grant or refuse the order.

(B.C. cont'd)

6.   The order will not be issued unless the child has lived with the prospective adoptive parents for at least six months.

When is the order generally issued?
Eight to ten months after placement.

Government Contact

Which government department or ministry is responsible for adoptions?
Ministry of Social Services. Contact:
Adoption Section
Family and Children Services
Ministry of Social Services
614 Humboldt Street
Victoria, British Columbia
Tel: (604) 387-3660
Fax: (604) 356-7862

How does this government department help individual prospective adoptive parents?

1.   Produces various adoption information pamphlets. Of particular interest is the booklet *Adoption General Information*.
2.   Prospective adoptive parents are generally referred to the government funded Adoptive Parents Association of British Columbia (contact information in Appendix I) to answer questions and receive the information pamphlets.

MANITOBA

Public Adoptions

What public agency processes public adoptions?
A local Child and Family Services Agency arranges public adoptions for members of its community.
Contact: Check local telephone book or call the government department responsible for adoptions listed below.

What is the estimated wait to adopt a newborn (who does not have special needs) through a public agency?[1]
Up to nine years.

Private Adoptions—General

What types of private adoption are available?[2]

1. Licensee Adoptions: No.
2. Independent Adoptions: Yes.
3. Identified Adoptions: No.

What adoption expenses and fees may prospective adoptive parents pay?[3]

1. Cannot give or agree to give any payment or reward, either directly or indirectly, (i) in consideration for the adoption of a child, or (ii) to procure or assist in procuring a child for the purpose of adoption.
2. Reasonable remuneration for professional services may, however, be paid to a lawyer acting for any party involved.

What other general information about private adoption should prospective adoptive parents know?

Only an *adult* (eighteen years of age or older) birth parent may place a child for purposes of adoption. If the birth mother is a minor (or the birth father, if he is required to consent to the adoption), the prospective adoptive parents may only obtain a guardianship order. A *de facto* adoption (no consent required by the birth parents) may then be completed after the child has lived with the prospective adoptive parents for three years.

Independent Adoptions

A. The Search

Which of the search methods discussed in Part II of this book may prospective adoptive parents use to find their child themselves?

1. Networking: Yes. Anyone who helps bring together the prospective adoptive and birth parents will be interviewed. Hard questions—why did you pick these parents, what will you tell an adopted child who comes to you—have caused some professionals to refuse to help.
2. Advertising: Yes. However, a newspaper or magazine published in Manitoba must receive approval in writing from the Director of Child and Family Services (the "Director") to

(Man. cont'd)

publish an advertisement dealing with adoption. Generally, an advertisement of a prospective adoptive parent will be permitted if it does not discuss any issue relating to money. For example, an advertisement cannot say "affluent couple looking to adopt."
3.   Mailings: Yes.

B. The Consent

Who must consent to the adoption?[4]

1.   The consent to adoption must be signed by both birth parents or the birth mother alone if she is (i) unmarried or (ii) married but ceased cohabiting with her husband 300 days or more before the child was born.
2.   As discussed below, (i) an adoption order will not be issued if an application has been filed to declare a man the father of the child until the application is withdrawn or dismissed and (ii) the birth father (whether or not entitled to consent) must be notified of the adoption hearing date. It may therefore be advisable to, whenever possible, obtain the consent of anyone who may be considered the birth father (signed certificate of live birth, etc.).
3.   See discussion under Private Adoptions—General with respect to birth parents under the age of majority.

When and how may the consent be signed?

1.   The consent may not be signed until the expiration of at least ten clear days after the date of the birth of the child.
2.   A lawyer, notary public or commissioner for oaths must witness the signing of the consent. The witness must swear an affidavit stating he or she (i) was personally present and saw the consent signed and (ii) knows the said person who in their belief is of the full age of eighteen years.[5]

When and how may the consent be withdrawn?
Up until the adoption order is issued, by written notice to the Director.

C. The Placement

What approvals and notifications are required before a child is placed in the prospective adoptive parents' home?

1. At least ten juridical days (Monday through Friday excluding statutory holidays) before the placement, the prospective adoptive parents must give their local public agency a *notice of intent to receive a child*. Similarly, the birth parents must submit a *notice of intent to place a child* to the public agency that serves the area where the prospective adoptive parents live. These notices must include the full names of the prospective adoptive and birth parents. Therefore, the parties are aware of each other's full names.[7]

2. The child cannot be placed with the prospective adoptive parents before the expiration of at least ten clear days after the date of the birth of the child. Generally, the child goes from the hospital to a family acceptable to both the prospective adoptive parents and the birth parents. This family is often friends or relatives of the prospective adoptive parents.

What other placement information should prospective adoptive parents know?

1. Upon receiving the placement notification, the local public agency will conduct an investigation. This investigation includes a review of the circumstances of the match, a homestudy, criminal record and child abuse registry checks and obtaining reference letters and medical examinations.

2. The birth parents remain the guardians of the child until the adoption order is issued.[8]

D. The Adoption Order

When and how is the adoption order obtained?

1. An adoption order is issued by a judge of the Court of Queen's Bench after a hearing. The prospective adoptive parents request a hearing by filing an application for an adoption order with the court.[9]

2. The application must be filed no earlier than six months and no later than twelve months from the date of placement.

(Man. cont'd)

3. Thirty days before the date fixed for the hearing of the application, the prospective adoptive parents must give the Director a copy of the consent to adoption.
4. Fourteen days before the date fixed for the hearing of the application, the prospective adoptive parents must give a copy of the application to (i) their local public agency, (ii) anyone who was required to consent to the adoption, and (iii) generally, the birth father even if he was not required to consent to the adoption.
5. The application must be supported by, among other items, a report of the investigation of the placement with a recommendation to grant the order and a certification of the Director that he has not been served with a notice of an application by a man that he be declared to be the father of the child.

When is the order generally issued?
Six to twelve months after placement.

Government Contact

Which government department or ministry is responsible for adoptions?
Department of Family Services. Contact:
Adoptions
Child and Family Support
114 Garry Street
Winnipeg, Manitoba
R3C 1G1
Tel: (204) 945-6962
Fax: (204) 945-6717

How does this government department help individual prospective adoptive parents?

1. Answers general questions about either private or public adoption—although a local public agency may be more helpful with respect to procedural questions.
2. Produces and distributes adoption pamphlet entitled *Adoption*.
3. Refers prospective adoptive parents to the appropriate local public agency.

NEW BRUNSWICK

Public Adoptions

What public agency processes public adoptions?
  A regional office of the Department of Health and Community
  Services arranges public adoptions for members of its community.
  Contact: Check local telephone book or call the Department of
          Health and Community Services, Adoption Services,
          listed below.

*What is the estimated wait to adopt a newborn (who does not have
special needs) through a public agency?*[1]
  Approximately eight years.

Private Adoptions — General

What types of private adoption are available?[2]

1.   Licensee Adoptions: No.
2.   Independent Adoptions: Yes.
3.   Identified Adoptions: No.

*What adoption expenses and fees may prospective adoptive parents
pay?*[3]
  The legislation is very strict. Basically, no direct or indirect payments can be made to anyone in relation to the adoption or proposed adoption of a child. However, government policy permits
  lawyers to be paid reasonable fees for completing the necessary
  legal steps.

*What other general information about private adoption should prospec-
tive adoptive parents know?*
  Private adoption procedures are currently being reviewed by the
  government. There may be changes to the legislation based on
  findings of this review.

(N.B. cont'd)

Independent Adoptions

A. The Search

Which of the search methods discussed in Part II of this book may prospective adoptive parents use to find their child themselves?

1.   Networking: Yes. However, no one other than the birth parents can contribute to the transfer of care of a child. Solicitation, negotiation and any act of assistance are considered contributing and, therefore, are prohibited.

 This requirement makes it very difficult for prospective adoptive parents to aggressively search for birth parents, since anyone they contact might be seen as contributing to the transfer of care of a child. Therefore, it is the birth parents who must do the looking. However, prospective adoptive parents may let people know they want to adopt a child and birth parents may generally be assisted in a minor way. For example, there should not be a problem in the following type of circumstance. Prospective adoptive parents tell a doctor they are trying to adopt. A pregnant patient asks the doctor if he can help her place her unborn child for adoption. The doctor tells the patient he knows people hoping to adopt and that if she wants he will tell her how to get in touch with them.
2.   Advertising: No.
3.   Mailings: No.

What other search information should prospective adoptive parents know?

 Since the legislation is very restrictive, prospective adoptive parents are very limited in how they can search and adopt within the province. Going outside of the province may be a better option.

B. The Consent

Who must consent to the adoption?[4]

1.   The consent to adoption must be signed by a *Parent* of the child to be adopted. The birth mother is always considered a Parent. The birth father will generally be considered a Parent if he (i) is married to the birth mother, (ii) has signed the birth registration form, (iii) has filed, with the birth mother, a declaration naming him the father, (iv) has been named the

father of the child in a court order, or (v) is a person with whom the child ordinarily resides who has demonstrated a settled intention to treat the child as a child of his family.

2. The legislation suggests that only one Parent need sign the consent. This resulted in the birth mother being the only Parent considered. A recent situation has caused the authorities to be more concerned with the birth father's rights.

3. Birth parents who are under the age of majority may still consent to the adoption.

When and how may the consent be signed?

1. Anytime after the birth of the child but it has no effect until the child is more than seven days old.

2. Anyone may witness the signing of the consent. The witness must swear an affidavit in the required form.[5]

When and how may the consent be withdrawn?
Anytime before the adoption order is issued, by written notice to the prospective adoptive parents or their lawyer.

C. The Placement

What approvals and notifications are required before a child is placed in the prospective adoptive parents' home?

1. No government approvals or notifications are required.

2. If the birth mother gives her permission, the child may be placed with the prospective adoptive parents directly from the hospital before the consent to adoption is signed. The exact procedure varies depending on the hospital. Sometimes the birth mother must leave the hospital with the child and then hand the child to the prospective adoptive parents' lawyer.

What is required immediately after the placement?

1. Within fifteen days of the placement, the prospective adoptive parents and the birth parents must notify the Minister of the Department of Health and Community Services (the "Minister") of the placement.[7]

2. Upon receiving the notification, the Minister will instigate an investigation of the placement. This investigation is conducted by a social worker employed by the local public agency

(N.B. cont'd)

and includes a review of the circumstances of the match, a homestudy and obtaining reference letters and medical examinations.

3. The Minister will provide the prospective adoptive parents and the birth parents a report of the investigation of the placement with a recommendation to grant or refuse the order.

D. The Adoption Order

When and how is the adoption order obtained?

1. An adoption order is issued by a judge of the Court of Queen's Bench after a successful hearing. The prospective adoptive parents request a hearing by filing an application for an adoption order with the court.[9]
2. The application may be filed after the child has lived continuously with the prospective adoptive parents for six months.
3. At least thirty days before filing the application, the prospective adoptive parents must notify the Minister of their intention to file the application.
4. Unless waived by the Minister, not later than ten days before the date fixed for the hearing of the application, the prospective adoptive parents must give the Minister notice of the hearing date and a copy of the application.

When is the order generally issued?
About seven months after placement.

Government Contact

Which government department or ministry is responsible for adoptions?
Department of Health and Community Services. Contact:
Adoption Service
Department of Health and Community Services
P.O. Box 5100
Fredericton, New Brunswick E3B 5G8
Tel: (506) 453-3830
Fax: (506) 453-2082

How does this government department help individual prospective adoptive parents?

1. Answers general questions about either private or public adoption. However, a local public agency may be more helpful with

respect to procedural questions and should therefore be contacted first.
2.   Produces an adoption pamphlet that is distributed by the local public agencies.

NEWFOUNDLAND

Public Adoptions

What public agency processes public adoptions?
A local office of the Department of Social Services arranges public adoptions for members of its community.
Contact: Check local telephone book or call the Department of Social Services, Adoptions, listed below.

What is the estimated wait to adopt a newborn (who does not have special needs) through a public agency?[1]
Eight to ten years.

Private Adoptions—General

What types of private adoption are available?[2]

1.   Licensee Adoptions: No.
2.   Independent Adoptions: Yes.
3.   Identified Adoptions: No.

What adoption expenses and fees may prospective adoptive parents pay?[3]
Cannot give or agree to give any payment or reward, directly or indirectly, (i) in consideration of the adoption of a child, or (ii) to obtain a child for the purpose of adoption.

What other general information about private adoption should prospective adoptive parents know?
In the past, the Department of Social Services (the "Department") has not condoned private adoption. This position has been successfully challenged in court. The current stance is in a state of flux.

(Nfld. cont'd)

Independent Adoptions

A. The Search

Which of the search methods discussed in Part II of this book may prospective adoptive parents use to find their child themselves?

1. Networking: No.
2. Advertising: No.
3. Mailings: No.

Other than the payment restriction stipulated above, there are no specific searching prohibitions in the legislation. However, as discussed below, approval of the Director of Child Welfare (the "Director") is required before a child may be placed in the home of prospective adoptive parents. It is currently the Director's position that aggressive searching by prospective adoptive parents will not be supported. Intermediaries such as doctors, lawyers or clergy may not be used. However, support will be given to birth parents who wish to select a couple for their child based on some previous relationship.

What other search information should prospective adoptive parents know?

Since the legislation is very restrictive, prospective adoptive parents are very limited in how they can search and adopt within the province. Going outside of the province may be a better option.

B. The Consent

Who must consent to the adoption?[4]

1. The consent to adoption must generally be signed by (i) each parent of the child to be adopted whose name appears on the record of birth, (ii) each person who has been declared, or applied to be declared, a parent by a court.
2. Birth parents who are under the age of nineteen may still consent to the adoption.

When and how may the consent be signed?

1. The consent may not be signed until the child is seven days old.
2. The signing of the consent is normally witnessed by a social worker employed by the Department.

When and how may the consent be withdrawn?
Within twenty-one days of signing, by written notice to the Director.

C. The Placement

What approvals and notifications are required before a child is placed in the prospective adoptive parents' home?

1. The Director must approve the placement. The prospective adoptive parents apply for approval by filling out an application with the Department.[7]
2. The Director's approval is based on an investigation conducted by a social worker employed by the Department. This investigation generally includes a review of the circumstances of the match, a homestudy, police checks and obtaining reference letters and medical examinations.

What is required immediately after the placement?
Rather than considering the placement an adoption placement, the Director may decide to consider it a foster placement. In these circumstances a foster home licence is issued and progress reports are required.

What other placement information should prospective adoptive parents know?

1. If the birth mother signs a non-ward agreement, the child may be placed with the prospective adoptive parents directly from the hospital before the consent to adoption is signed.
2. The Director is the guardian of the child during the interval after the twenty-one day period for withdrawing the consent has elapsed and before the issuance of the adoption order.[8]

D. The Adoption Order

When and how is the adoption order obtained?

1. An adoption order is issued by a judge of the Trial Division or Provincial Court after a successful hearing. The prospective adoptive parents, or a social worker employed by the Department, request a hearing by filing an application for an adoption order with the judge.[9]

(Nfld. cont'd)

2. The Director must (i) issue a Director's certificate in order to proceed to court and (ii) be represented (usually by a social worker employed by the Department) at the hearing.
3. The order will not be issued unless the child has lived with the prospective adoptive parents for at least six months.

When is the order generally issued?
Eight to ten months after placement.

Government Contact

Which government department or ministry is responsible for adoptions?
Department of Social Services. Contact:
Adoptions
Department of Social Services
3rd Floor, West Block
Confederation Building
Box 8700
St. John's, Newfoundland A1B 4J6
Tel: (709) 729-3899
Fax: (709) 729-0583

How does this government department help individual prospective adoptive parents?

1. Answers general questions about either private or public adoption, although a local public agency provides direct client service.
2. Currently producing an adoption pamphlet.

NORTHWEST TERRITORIES

Public Adoptions

What public agency processes public adoptions?
A local office of the Department of Social Services arranges public adoptions for members of its community.
Contact: Check local telephone book or call the Department of Social Services, Child Welfare and Adoption, listed below.

What is the estimated wait to adopt a newborn (who does not have special needs) through a public agency?[1]

Have not accepted an application in eight years.

Private Adoptions—General

What types of private adoption are available?[2]

1. Licensee Adoptions: No.
2. Independent Adoptions: Yes.
3. Identified Adoptions: No.

What adoption expenses and fees may prospective adoptive parents pay?[3]

1. Cannot give or agree to give any payment or reward, either directly or indirectly, to procure or assist in procuring a child for the purposes of adoption.
2. There is no stipulation of the type of payments which may be made by prospective adoptive parents. Paying expenses of the birth parents may be considered "giving an indirect payment" and should only be done with respect to expenses such as reasonable counselling and legal fees.

Independent Adoptions

A. The Search

Which of the search methods discussed in Part II of this book may prospective adoptive parents use to find their child themselves?

1. Networking: Yes.
2. Advertising: No.
3. Mailings: Yes.

B. The Consent

Who must consent to the adoption?[4]

1. The consent to adoption must be signed by each *Guardian* of the child to be adopted. The term "Guardian" is not defined by the legislation. Generally, the consent of both the birth parents is required unless a judge dispenses with a required consent. *(N.W.T. cont'd)*

2. A birth parent who is under the age of majority may still con-
    sent to the adoption. However, the birth grandparents must
    then sign the consent as well.

When and how may the consent be signed?

1. The consent may not be signed by the birth mother until after
    the expiration of four days from the date of birth of the child.
    Generally, the birth father signs the consent at the same time
    as the birth mother.
2. The birth parents should have independent legal advice prior
    to signing the consent.
3. Any third party may witness the signing of the consent and
    sign an affidavit stating they witnessed it.[5]

When and how may the consent be withdrawn?

Consents cannot be withdrawn unless it is shown to the court's
satisfaction that it is in the best interests of the child.[6]

C. The Placement

*What approvals and notifications are required before a child is placed
in the prospective adoptive parents' home?*

1. No government approvals or notifications are required.
2. If the birth mother signs a release form, the child may be
    placed with the prospective adoptive parents directly from the
    hospital before the consent to adoption is signed.

What is required immediately after the placement?

Within thirty days of the placement, the prospective adoptive parents and the birth parents must notify the Superintendent of Child
Welfare (the "Superintendent") of the transfer of custody.[7]

*What other placement information should prospective adoptive par-
ents know?*

Generally, the birth parents sign an interim custody agreement
giving the prospective adoptive parents guardianship of the child.
Otherwise, the birth parents remain the guardians until the adoption order is issued.[8]

D. The Adoption Order

When and how is the adoption order obtained?

1. An adoption order is issued by a judge of the Supreme Court of the Northwest Territories after a successful hearing.
2. The prospective adoptive parents begin the process by submitting an application for an adoption order to the Superintendent.
3. Upon receiving the application, the Superintendent will instigate an investigation of the placement. This investigation is generally conducted by a child welfare worker employed by the Department of Social Services and includes a review of the circumstances of the match, a homestudy and obtaining reference letters and medical examinations.
4. Within one year after the placement, the Superintendent will present a petition for an adoption order to the judge.[9]
5. The order will not be issued unless the child has lived with the prospective adoptive parents for at least six months.

When is the order generally issued?
One year after placement.

Government Contact

Which government department or ministry is responsible for adoptions?
Department of Social Services. Contact:
Child Welfare and Adoption
Department of Social Services
Government of the Northwest Territories
4920 52nd Street
Yellowknife, Northwest Territories X1A 3T1
Tel: (403) 920-8920
Fax: (403) 873-0317

How does this government department help individual prospective adoptive parents?
Answers general questions about either private or public adoption, although a local public agency may be more helpful with respect to procedural questions.

NOVA SCOTIA

Public Adoptions

What public agency processes public adoptions?
A local Children's Aid Society, Family and Children's Services Agency, District Office of the Department of Community Services or approved child-placing agency arranges public adoptions for members of its community.
Contact: Check local telephone book or call the Department of Community Services, Family and Children's Services Division listed below.

What is the estimated wait to adopt a newborn (who does not have special needs) through a public agency?[1]
Up to ten years.

Private Adoptions—General

What types of private adoption are available?[2]

1. Licensee Adoptions: No.
2. Independent Adoptions: Yes.
3. Identified Adoptions: No.

What adoption expenses and fees may prospective adoptive parents pay?[3]

1. Cannot give any payment, directly or indirectly, (i) in consideration of the placement for adoption of a child, or (ii) to procure a child for the purpose of adoption.
2. There is no stipulation of the type of payments which may be made by prospective adoptive parents. Paying expenses of the birth parents may be considered "giving an indirect payment" and should only be done with respect to expenses such as reasonable legal fees.

What other general information about private adoption should prospective adoptive parents know?
An Advisory Committee of the Legislature has submitted a report recommending various changes to the adoption legislation. The most relevant suggestion is that a homestudy be required before the child is placed in the prospective adoptive parent's home.

Independent Adoptions

A. The Search

Which of the search methods discussed in Part II of this book may prospective adoptive parents use to find their child themselves?
1.   Networking: Yes.
2.   Advertising: Yes.
3.   Mailings: Yes.

B. The Consent

Who must consent to the adoption?[4]

1.   The consent to adoption must be signed by each *Parent* of the child to be adopted. The birth mother is always considered a Parent. The birth father will generally be considered a Parent if (i) the child is legitimate or legitimated, (ii) he has acknowledged paternity of the child and has an application before a court respecting custody, support or access for the child at the time proceedings for adoption are commenced, or (iii) he has acknowledged paternity of the child and has provided support for or exercised access to the child at any time during the two years before proceedings for adoption are commenced.
2.   In addition, an individual may be considered a Parent if he or she: (i) has custody of the child, (ii) during the twelve months before proceedings for adoption are commenced, has stood in *loco parentis* to the child (see below), or (iii) under court order or written agreement, is required to provide support for the child or has a right of access to the child and has, at any time during the two years before proceedings for adoption are commenced, provided support or exercised a right of access.
3.   An individual stands in *loco parentis* to a child when he or she (i) cohabits with a member of the opposite sex who is the father or mother of the child and who has the care of that child, (ii) contributes to the financial support of the child, and (iii) behaves towards the child as if the child was the son or daughter of the individual.
4.   Birth parents who are under the age of majority may still consent to the adoption.

(N.S. cont'd)

When and how may the consent be signed?

1. The consent may be signed not less than fifteen clear days after the birth of the child.
2. Before signing a consent, a Parent must receive professional counselling from a person approved by the Minister of Community Services (the "Minister"). The approved person will be an employee of the local public agency.

When and how may the consent be withdrawn?

The consent cannot be withdrawn unless it is shown to the court's satisfaction that it is in the best interests of the child.[6]

C. The Placement

What approvals and notifications are required before a child is placed in the prospective adoptive parents' home?

1. The prospective adoptive parents must notify their local public agency of the intent to adopt.[7]
2. A person approved by the Minister must complete the required counselling and a social and medical history of the birth parents.
3. The child cannot be placed with the prospective adoptive parents before the consent to adoption is signed. Generally, the child goes from the hospital to a family acceptable to both the prospective adoptive parents and the birth parents. This family is often friends or relatives of the prospective adoptive parents.

What is required immediately after the placement?

1. Within ten days of the placement, the prospective adoptive parents must notify the Minister of the proposed adoption.
2. Upon receipt of the notification, the Minister will instigate an investigation of the placement. This investigation is generally conducted by the local public agency and includes a homestudy, police and child abuse register checks and obtaining reference letters.

D. The Adoption Order

When and how is the adoption order obtained?

1. An adoption order is issued by a judge of the Supreme Court after a successful hearing. The prospective adoptive parents

request a hearing by filing an application for an adoption order with the court.[9]

2. The application may be filed after the child has lived with the prospective adoptive parents for six months.
3. One month before the date fixed for the hearing of the application, the prospective adoptive parents must give the Minister notice of the hearing date and a copy of the application.
4. Before the hearing, the Minister will provide the lawyer representing the prospective adoptive parents a recommendation to grant or refuse the order. The recommendation is then filed with the court.

When is the order generally issued?
Varies between six to ten months after placement.

Government Contact

Which government department or ministry is responsible for adoptions?
Department of Community Services. Contact:
Department of Community Services
Family and Children's Services Division
P.O. Box 696, 5182 Prince Street
Halifax, Nova Scotia
B3J 2T7
Tel: (902) 424-3205
Fax: (902) 424-0502

How does this government department help individual prospective adoptive parents?

1. Answers general questions about either private or public adoption.
2. Produces a brochure entitled *Thinking of Adopting*.
3. Will provide, for a fee, the legal services necessary to obtain the adoption order.

ONTARIO

Public Adoptions

What public agency arranges public adoptions?
   Generally, a local Children's Aid Society arranges public adoptions for members of its community. However, in certain communities there is a further division by religion. For example, the Catholic community in Metropolitan Toronto, Hamilton and Windsor are served by branches of the Catholic Children's Aid Society and the Jewish community in Metropolitan Toronto is served by the Jewish Family and Child Service of Metropolitan Toronto.
   Contact: Check local telephone book or call the government department responsible for adoptions listed below.

What is the estimated wait to adopt a newborn (who does not have special needs) through a public agency?[1]
   Varies greatly depending on the public agency. However, such an adoption is rare since most of the children available for adoption have special needs.

Private Adoptions—General

What types of private adoption are available?[2]

1.   Licensee Adoptions: Yes.
2.   Independent Adoptions: No.
3.   Identified Adoptions: Yes.

What adoption expenses and fees may prospective adoptive parents pay?[3]

1.   Cannot give or agree to give any payment or reward of any kind in connection with (i) a child's adoption or placement for adoption, (ii) a consent to the child's adoption, or (iii) negotiations or arrangements with a view to the child's adoption.
2.   Certain defined expenses of a licensee and proper legal fees and disbursements may, however, be paid.

Identified Adoptions

A. The Search

Which of the search methods discussed in Part II of this book may prospective adoptive parents use to find their child themselves?

1. Networking: Yes.
2. Advertising: Yes.
3. Mailings: Yes.

B. The Consent

Who must consent to the adoption?[4]

1. The consent to adoption must be signed by each *Parent* of the child to be adopted. The birth mother is always considered a Parent. Unless it is proved on a balance of probabilities that he is not the child's birth father, an individual will generally be considered a Parent if he: (i) is married to the birth mother at the time of the birth of the child, (ii) was married to the mother by a marriage terminated within 300 days before the birth, (iii) marries the birth mother after the birth and acknowledges that he is the birth father, (iv) was cohabiting with the birth mother in a relationship of some permanence at the time of the birth or the child is born within 300 days after they ceased to cohabit, (v) has certified the child's birth, as the child's birth father, under the relevant legislation, (vi) has been found or recognized by a Canadian court to be the birth father.
2. In addition, an individual may be considered a Parent if he or she: (i) has lawful custody of the child, (ii) during the twelve months before the child is placed for adoption, has demonstrated a settled intention to treat the child as a child of his or her family, or has acknowledged parentage of the child and provided for the child's support, (iii) under court order or written agreement, is required to provide support for the child, has custody of the child or has a right of access to the child, (iv) has filed a statutory declaration acknowledging parentage of the child.

When and how may the consent be signed?

1. A consent may not be signed before (i) the child is a full seven days old, (ii) the licensee has advised the Parents of their rights, and (iii) the Parents have been given the opportunity to seek counselling and independent legal advice.
2. An employee of the local Children's Aid Society must witness the signing of the consent.

(Ont. cont'd)

3. A representative of the Official Guardian must meet with any Parent who is under eighteen years old to ensure that they understand their rights and that signing the consent reflects their true wishes.

When and how may the consent be withdrawn?
Not later than twenty-one days after the signing, by written notice to a Children's Aid Society or to the court office identified on the consent.

C. The Placement

What approvals and notifications are required before a child is placed in the prospective adoptive parents' home?

1. The Director of the Ministry of Community and Social Services (the "Director") must approve the placement.
2. Approval by the Director is based on the following, provided to the Director by the licensee working with the prospective adoptive parents: homestudy report, medical history and reference letters of the prospective adoptive parents and social and medical history of the birth parents. The homestudy or an update must have been completed within six months of the placement by a social worker approved by the Ministry to do homestudies. In addition, the licensee must assure the Director that the adoptive parents are the choice of the birth parents; the birth parents must have discussed a number of prospective adoptive parents or understand they have that option.
3. With the permission of the birth parents, the child may be placed with the prospective adoptive parents directly from the hospital before the consent to adoption is signed. However, many licensees prefer to have the child remain in the hospital or, when necessary, be placed in a temporary foster home until the consent is signed.

What is required immediately after the placement?
Within thirty days of the placement, (i) the prospective adoptive parents must provide a written acknowledgement of the placement to the licensee, and (ii) the licensee must file a copy of this acknowledgement as well as their own notice of the placement with the Director.

What other placement information should prospective adoptive parents know?

The licensee is the guardian of the child during the interval after the twenty-one day period for withdrawing the consent has elapsed and before the issuance of the adoption order.[8]

D. The Adoption Order

When and how is the adoption order obtained?

1. An adoption order is issued by a judge of the Provincial Court (Family Division) or the Unified Family Court after a successful hearing. The prospective adoptive parents request a hearing by filing an application for an adoption order with the court.[7,9]
2. The application may be filed after the child has lived with the prospective adoptive parents for six months.
3. Before the hearing, the Director will file a statement with the court indicating that it is in the best interests of the child for the order to be given. The Director's statement is based on a report of the child's adjustment in the prospective adoptive parents' home. This report is prepared by an approved social worker, usually the same one who conducted the homestudy, and is based on one visit within the first month of the placement and at least two more visits.
4. If the adoption order is not issued within one year of either the placement or the signing of the consent, the licensee must supply reasons to the Director.

When is the order generally issued?

Eight to ten months after placement.

Government Contact

Which government department or ministry is responsible for adoptions?

Ministry of Community and Social Services. Contact:
Adoption Unit
Ministry of Community and Social Services
2 Bloor Street West, 24th Floor
Toronto, Ontario M7A 1E9
Tel: (416) 327-4730
Fax: (416) 327-0573

(Ont. cont'd)

How does this government department help individual prospective adoptive parents?

1. Answers general questions about either private or public adoption, although a local public agency may be more helpful with respect to procedural questions about public adoptions.
2. Produces and distributes various information pamphlets. Of particular interest are the booklets *How to Adopt in Ontario*, *Are you thinking of adoption for your child*, and *Information about International Adoption*.
3. Supplies lists of licensees and social workers approved to do private adoption homestudies.

PRINCE EDWARD ISLAND

Public Adoptions

What public agency processes public adoptions?
The Health and Community Services Agency arranges public adoptions for residents of the province. Two Family Service Agencies [Catholic Family Services Bureau, Charlottetown (902-894-8591) and Prince County Family Service Bureau in Summerside (902-436-9171)] also have the ability to process public adoptions. However, neither Agency has been active in adoptions in the last few years.
Contact: Check local telephone book or call Adoption Services of the Health and Community Services Agency listed below.

What is the estimated wait to adopt a newborn (who does not have special needs) through a public agency?[1]
Six years.

Private Adoptions—General

What types of private adoption are available?[2]

1. Licensee Adoptions: Yes, through a *Private Agent*.
2. Independent Adoptions: No.
3. Identified Adoptions: Yes.

What adoption expenses and fees may prospective adoptive parents pay?[3]

1. Cannot give or agree to give any payment or reward, either directly or indirectly to procure or assist in procuring a child for the purposes of placement or adoption.
2. The restriction does not preclude payments (i) to reimburse for reasonable costs incurred, (ii) for services of the Director of Child Welfare (the "Director"), (iii) for Director approved or authorized services of a Private Agent or Family Service Agency, and (iv) to a lawyer, within a range considered reasonable by the Law Society of P.E.I. for the services given.

Identified Adoptions

A. The Search

Which of the search methods discussed in Part II of this book may prospective adoptive parents use to find their child themselves?

1. Networking: Yes.
2. Advertising: Yes.
3. Mailings: Yes.

B. The Consent

Who must consent to the adoption?[4]

1. The consent to adoption must be signed by the birth mother. The birth father must also sign the consent if (i) he is married to the birth mother, (ii) registered as the father under the relevant legislation, or (iii) his paternity has been legally established under the relevant legislation.
2. Birth parents who are under the age of majority may still consent to the adoption.

When and how may the consent be signed?

1. Once the child is fourteen days old, the consent to adoption may be signed.
2. A social worker authorized by the Director or a lawyer must witness the signing of the consent to adoption. The witness must ensure that the person signing the consent (i) has

(P.E.I. cont'd)

received an explanation of the effects of adoption, (ii) has had the opportunity, or is aware of the option, of obtaining the advice of a lawyer, (iii) has had the opportunity, or is aware of the option, of obtaining counselling support, and (iv) appears to make the decision freely and voluntarily.

When and how may the consent be withdrawn?
Within fourteen days of having signed the consent, by written notice to the prospective adoptive parents and the Director.

C. The Placement

What approvals and notifications are required before a child is placed in the prospective adoptive parents' home?

1. Generally before the placement, a homestudy or *assessment of placement risk* must be conducted by a social worker authorized by the Director. The Private Agent must notify the Director of the placement and of the results of the assessment.
2. After the birth and before the placement, a consent to placement must be signed. The same people required to sign the consent to adoption must sign this consent.
3. Prior to signing the consent to placement, a social worker authorized by the Director must (i) provide the birth parents with placement counselling, and (ii) inform the birth parents of their right to obtain independent legal advice.
4. Where it is possible to identify and contact the person who is apparently the birth father, even though he does not have a clear entitlement to consent, the Private Agent working with the prospective adoptive parents generally makes all reasonable efforts to (i) inform the presumed birth father that placement and adoption are intended, (ii) explain to him the provisions concerning establishing paternity, entitlement to placement counselling and consenting to placement and adoption, and (iii) offer him the opportunity to sign a declaration to record that he has been so informed and that he does not wish to pursue or exercise entitlement to consent.

What is required immediately after the placement?

1. Within one month of the placement, the Private Agent must supply background and placement information about the child to the Director.

2. The Private Agent must monitor the placement. The monitoring includes visits at least once during the first month and subsequently no less frequently than once every two months until pre-hearing adoption study is begun (see below).

What other placement information should prospective adoptive parents know?

After the child is fourteen days old, the birth parents may sign a guardianship agreement, either full or partial, making the prospective adoptive parents the guardians of the child. Otherwise, the Director is the guardian until the adoption order is issued.[8]

D. The Adoption Order

When and how is the adoption order obtained?

1. An adoption order is issued by a judge of the Family Section of the Trial Division of the Supreme Court of P.E.I. after a successful hearing. The prospective adoptive parents request a hearing by filing an application for an adoption order with the court.[7,9]
2. The application may be filed after the child has lived with the prospective adoptive parents for three months.
3. Ten days before the date fixed for the hearing of the application, the prospective adoptive parents must arrange for a pre-hearing adoption study to be provided to the court. The study must have been completed or updated within the six-month period preceding the hearing by the Director, a Family Service Agency or a social worker authorized by the Director. The study provides information concerning the suitability of the placement and must consist of at least three observations over a period of at least one month.
4. The hearing must be within a year of the signing of the consent to adoption, otherwise the consent expires.

When is the order generally issued?

Six to seven months after placement.

(P.E.I. cont'd)

Government Contact

Which government department or ministry is responsible for adoptions?

Health and Community Services Agency. Contact:
Adoption Services
Health and Community Services Agency
P.O. Box 2000
Charlottetown, P.E.I. C1A 7N8
Tel: (902) 368-6511
Fax: (902) 368-6136

How does this government department help individual prospective adoptive parents?

1. Answers general questions about either private or public adoption.
2. Produces and distributes an adoption pamphlet entitled *Adoption on Prince Edward Island.*
3. Supplies lists of Private Agents and social workers approved to do placement counselling, assessment of placement risk, placement monitoring, pre-hearing adoption studies and to obtain consents.

QUEBEC

Public Adoptions

What public agency processes public adoptions?
A local Youth Protection Centre or Youth Centre arranges public adoptions for members of its community.
Contact: Check local telephone book or call:
Association des centres jeunesse du Québec
2000 rue Mansfield, bureau 400
Montréal, Québec H3A 2Z1
Tel: (514) 842-5181
Fax: (414) 842-4834

What is the estimated wait to adopt a newborn (who does not have special needs) through a public agency?
Longer than eight years.

Private Adoptions—General

What types of private adoption are available?

1. The private adoption of a child born or living in Quebec is not permitted.
2. The private adoption of a child born or living outside Quebec may be facilitated through contacts established by the prospective adoptive parents in the jurisdiction outside of Quebec or through a private agency certified by the Minister of Health and Social Services. Generally, the private agencies only act as intermediaries with adoption authorities of other countries.

What adoption expenses and fees may prospective adoptive parents pay?
Must comply with the requirements of the jurisdiction where the child to be adopted is born or lives.

What other general information about private adoption should prospective adoptive parents know?
The adoption order must be either (i) issued in Quebec, or (ii) issued outside of Quebec and then recognized by a Quebec court.

Independent Adoptions of a Child Born outside Quebec

A. The Search

The search requirements are determined by the jurisdiction where the child to be adopted will be born.

B. The Consent

The consent requirements are determined by the jurisdiction where the child to be adopted was born.

C. The Placement

What approvals and notifications are required before a child is placed in the prospective adoptive parents' home?
A homestudy or *psychosocial assessment* must be completed. If the adoption order is to be issued in Quebec, the assessment must be completed by an employee of the Director of Youth Protection (the "Director") or a person licensed for that purpose by the Director.

(Que. cont'd)

If the adoption order is to be issued in another province, the assessment may be completed by a member of the Corporation professionnelle des psychlogues du Québec (Professional Psychologists of Quebec), 514-738-1881, or the Corporation professionnelle des travailleurs sociaux du Québec (Professional Social Workers of Quebec), 514-731-3925.

What other placement information should prospective adoptive parents know?

1. The child may be placed with the prospective adoptive parents when permitted by the laws of the jurisdiction where the child to be adopted was born. However, the child cannot be brought into Quebec until the Secrétariat à l'adoption internationale (the "Secretariat") issues a letter of authorization. To issue the letter, the Secretariat requires either (i) the birth certificate of the child and the consent to the adoption, (ii) the adoption order issued in the province where the child was born, or (iii) the authorization of the province where the child was born. The letter will not be issued unless the consent withdrawal period has elapsed.
2. The local Youth Protection Centre and the prospective adoptive parents are joint guardians of the child during the interval after any consent withdrawal period has elapsed and before the issuance of the adoption order.[8]

D. Obtaining an Adoption Order in Quebec

When and how is an adoption order obtained?

1. Before an adoption order or *adoption judgment* is issued, a judgment of placement must be issued. A judgment of placement is issued by a judge of the Youth Court after a successful hearing. A lawyer employed by either the local Youth Protection Centre or the prospective adoptive parents requests a hearing by filing an application for a judgment of placement with the court. Included in the application is a letter issued by the Secretariat stating that the prospective adoptive parents have complied with the relevant laws of Quebec and the province where the child was born.[9]
2. The adoption judgment is also issued by a judge of the Youth Court after a requested hearing. The court will grant the

judgment unless a progress report prepared by an employee of the Director indicates that the child has not adapted to the adopting family.

3. Generally, the adoption judgment will not be issued until six months after the judgment of placement has been issued.

When is the adoption judgment generally issued?
Eighteen months after the child is placed in the prospective adoptive parents' home. May be quicker if the prospective adoptive parents hire a lawyer in private practice rather than use a lawyer employed by the Director.

E. Recognizing an Adoption Order Obtained outside Quebec

When and how is an adoption order issued outside Quebec recognized by Quebec?

1. An adoption order is recognized by a judge of the Youth Court after a hearing. The prospective adoptive parents request a hearing by filing an application for recognition with the court.
2. The application may be filed any time after the child has been brought into Quebec and the adoption order has been issued.
3. The court must be satisfied that the rules respecting consent to adoption and eligibility for adoption in the other jurisdiction have been observed.

Government Contact

Which government department or ministry is responsible for adoptions?
Ministry of Health and Social Services. However, the Ministry has set up a separate government body to coordinate the adoption of children born outside of Quebec by those living in Quebec:
Secrétariat à l'adoption internationale
(International Adoption Secretariat)
3700, rue Berri
Montréal, Québec H2L 4G9
Tel: (514) 873-5226 or 1-800-561-0246
Fax: (514) 873-1709

How does this government department help individual prospective adoptive parents?

1. Answers general questions about adoption.

(Que. cont'd)

2. Distributes various government information pamphlets. Currently, there are several useful publications only available in French. The only publication available in English is *Notes on the Legislation of Quebec (Canada) Concerning International Adoption*. (An adoption of a child born outside of Quebec but inside Canada is governed by the same laws.)
3. Supplies lists of certified private agencies, adoptive parent support groups and adoption organizations.

SASKATCHEWAN

Public Adoptions

What public agency processes public adoptions?
A regional office of the Department of Social Services arranges public adoptions for members of its community.
Contact: Check local telephone book or call Adoption Services of the Department of Social Services, Family and Youth Services Division, listed below.

What is the estimated wait to adopt a newborn (who does not have special needs) through a public agency?[1]
Seven to ten years.

Private Adoptions—General

What types of private adoption are available?[2]

1. Licensee Adoptions: Yes.
2. Independent Adoptions: Yes.
3. Identified Adoptions: No.

What adoption expenses and fees may prospective adoptive parents pay?[3]

1. Unless otherwise permitted, cannot give or agree to give any payment or reward, whether directly or indirectly, for any purpose related to the adoption of a child.
2. Reasonable fees may generally be paid: (i) to an approved person for the preparation of a homestudy, (ii) to a translator, (iii) to a lawyer for legal fees in relation to obtaining an adop-

tion order unless the lawyer or a member of the lawyer's law firm was involved in the introduction of the birth and adoptive parents, (iv) to a person who provides required independent advice, (v) to a professional who provided medical reports, psychological assessments or related services, (vi) for actual cost of transportation related to the placement of the child, (vii) in the case of an international adoption, specific maintenance costs for a child, and (viii) for services provided by the government of Saskatchewan or a licensee.

What other general information about private adoption should prospective adoptive parents know?

Licensee adoptions are available through one *licensed agency* funded by government grant: the Christian Counselling Adoption Services in Saskatoon (306-244-9836). In mid-1993, the Agency closed its waiting list due to the large number of prospective adoptive parents on the list. The list is not expected to reopen until March of 1996.

Independent Adoptions

A. The Search

Which of the search methods discussed in Part II of this book may prospective adoptive parents use to find their child themselves?

1. Networking: Yes.
2. Advertising: No.
3. Mailings: Mailing a birth mother letter to unknown contacts, *cold letter mailings*, would probably be considered advertising and therefore not permitted. Mailing birth mother letters to referred contacts should not be considered advertising and therefore permitted.

What other search information should prospective adoptive parents know?

Residents of Saskatchewan who find a child to adopt who was born or lives outside of the province have notification requirements, even if the adoption is to be completed outside of the province (see "The Placement" below).

(Sask. cont'd)

B. The Consent

Who must consent to the adoption?[4]

1. The consent to adoption must be signed by the birth mother. The birth father must also sign the consent if he (i) at the time of the child's birth or conception was living with the birth mother, (ii) together with the birth mother, has registered the child's birth, (iii) has access to or custody of the child by court order or agreement, (iv) acknowledges that he is the birth father and has supported or maintained the child or the birth mother, or (v) has been declared by a court to be the father of the child pursuant to the relevant Saskatchewan legislation.
2. Where a question arises as to whether a person is the birth father of a child, that person may apply to the court for an order declaring him to be the birth father (i) prior to the child's birth, or (ii) within ten days of the birth.
3. Birth parents who are under the age of eighteen may still consent to the adoption.

When and how may the consent be signed?

1. The consent may not be signed until the child is three days old.
2. If only the birth mother signs the consent, she must sign an affidavit stating she is the child's only birth parent within the meaning of the law.[5]
3. A lawyer who does not represent the prospective adoptive parents must (i) explain to the birth parents signing the consent their rights with respect to withdrawing the consent and the effects of an adoption order, (ii) be satisfied that the consent represents the wishes of the birth parents, and (iii) complete a certificate of independent advice.

When and how may the consent be withdrawn?
Within fourteen days after the signing, by written notice to the Director of Family and Youth Services (the "Director").

C. The Placement

What approvals and notifications are required before a child is placed in the prospective adoptive parents' home?

1. No government approvals or notifications are required, unless the child lives or was born outside Saskatchewan. In such

circumstances, the Director must be notified thirty days before placement. The Director will want to ensure that the adoption is being regulated by one jurisdiction.[7]

2. Generally, the birth parents sign a custody agreement making the prospective adoptive parents the guardians of the child. Otherwise, the birth parents remain the guardians until the adoption order is issued.[8]

3. If guardianship is transferred, the child may be placed with the prospective adoptive parents directly from the hospital before the consent to adoption is signed.

D. The Adoption Order

When and how is the adoption order obtained?

1. An adoption order is issued by a judge of the Queen's Bench or the Unified Family Court after a successful hearing. The prospective adoptive parents request a hearing by filing an application for an adoption order with the court.[9]

2. The application may be filed at any time within one year of the date on which the child was placed in the prospective adoptive parents home. If the application is not filed within the year, and no extensions have been granted, new consents must be obtained from the birth parents.

3. Thirty days before filing the application, the prospective adoptive parents must give the Director a copy of the application.

4. Upon receiving the copy of the application, the Director may file any information relevant to the application with the court.

5. The supporting material that accompanies the application includes a homestudy completed by a person approved by the Director, medical and social history of the birth parents obtained by the prospective adoptive parents and information respecting the reason the child was placed for adoption with the prospective adoptive parents.

When is the order generally issued?
Six to sixteen weeks after placement.

(Sask. cont'd)

Government Contact

Which government department or ministry is responsible for adoptions?
Department of Social Services. Contact:
Adoption Services
Family and Youth Services Division
Department of Social Services
1920 Broad Street, 12th Floor
Regina, Saskatchewan S4P 3V6
Tel: (306) 787-5698
Fax: (306) 787-0925

How does this government department help individual prospective adoptive parents?

1. Answers general questions about either private or public adoption, although a local public agency may be more helpful with respect to procedural questions.
2. Produces and distributes adoption pamphlets and fact sheets.

YUKON TERRITORY

Public Adoptions

What public agency processes public adoptions?
A local office of the Department of Health and Social Services arranges public adoptions for members of its community.
Contact: Check local telephone book or call the Placement and Support Services Supervisor, Department of Health and Social Services, Family and Children Services, listed below.

What is the estimated wait to adopt a newborn (who does not have special needs) through a public agency?[1]
Such an adoption is rare since most of the children available for adoption through a public agency have special needs.

Private Adoptions—General

What types of private adoption are available?[2]

1. Licensee Adoptions: No.

2. Independent Adoptions: Yes.
3. Identified Adoptions: No.

What adoption expenses and fees may prospective adoptive parents pay?[3]

1. Cannot give, or attempt to give, any payment or benefit in return for (i) giving up a child or rights in relation to a child, or (ii) inducing a person to give up a child or rights in relation to a child.
2. There is no stipulation of the type of payments which may be made by prospective adoptive parents. Paying expenses of the birth parents may be considered "giving benefit" and should only be done with respect to expenses such as reasonable counselling and legal fees.

Independent Adoptions

A. The Search

Which of the search methods discussed in Part II of this book may prospective adoptive parents use to find their child themselves?

1. Networking: Yes.
2. Advertising: Yes.
3. Mailings: Yes.

B. The Consent

Who must consent to the adoption?[4]

1. Both the birth mother and the birth father must consent to the adoption. Unless the contrary is proven on the balance of probabilities, a person will generally be presumed to be the birth father if he: (i) is married to the birth mother at the time of the birth of the child, (ii) was married to the mother by a marriage terminated 300 days before the birth, (iii) marries the birth mother after the birth and acknowledges that he is the birth father, (iv) was cohabiting with the birth mother in a relationship of some permanence at the time of the birth or the child is born within 300 days after they ceased to cohabit, (v), and the birth mother have acknowledged in

(Yukon cont'd)

writing that he is the father of the child, (vi) has been found or recognized in his lifetime by a court to be the birth father.

2.   Birth parents who are under the age of majority may still consent to the adoption.

When and how may the consent be signed?

1.   The consent may be signed at any time.
2.   Anyone other than a government employee who reports to the Director of Family and Children Services (the "Director") may witness the signing of the consent. The witness must explain the nature and effect of the consent and certify that the person signing appears to understand the nature and effect and to sign it voluntarily.

When and how may the consent be withdrawn?

The consent may be withdrawn without giving reasons within thirty days of signing, by written notice to the Director. After the thirty-day period, the consent may only be withdrawn if it is shown to the court's satisfaction that it is in the best interests of the child.[6]

C. The Placement

What approvals and notifications are required before a child is placed in the prospective adoptive parents' home?

1.   No government approvals or notifications are required.
2.   Generally, the birth parents sign an agreement transferring guardianship of the child to the prospective adoptive parents. Otherwise, the birth parents remain the guardians until the adoption order is issued.[8]
3.   If guardianship is transferred or the birth parents consent to the adoption or sign a release form, the child may be placed with the prospective adoptive parents directly from the hospital.

What is required immediately after the placement?

1.   Within thirty days of the placement, the prospective adoptive parents and anyone who placed or facilitated the placement of the child must notify the Director of the intention to adopt the child.[7]

2. Upon receiving the notification, the Director will instigate an investigation. This investigation is generally conducted by a social worker employed by the Director and includes a review of the circumstances of the match, a homestudy, and obtaining reference letters and medical examinations.

D. The Adoption Order

When and how is the adoption order obtained?

1. An adoption order is issued by a judge of the Supreme Court of the Yukon after a successful hearing. The prospective adoptive parents request a hearing by filing a petition for an adoption order with the court.[9]
2. The Director must have received notice of the intention to adopt (see above) at least six months before the hearing date.
3. One month before the date fixed for the hearing of the petition, the prospective adoptive parents must give the Director notice of the hearing date and a copy of the petition.
4. Before the hearing, the Director will file with the court a report of the investigation of the placement with a recommendation to grant or refuse the order.
5. The order will not be issued unless the child has lived with the prospective adoptive parents for six months.

When is the order generally issued?
Eight to twelve months after placement.

Government Contact

Which government department or ministry is responsible for adoptions?
Department of Health and Social Services. Contact:
Placement and Support Services Supervisor
Department of Health and Social Services, H-10
Box 2703
Whitehorse, Yukon Y1A 2C6
Tel: (403) 667-3002
Fax: (403) 668-4613

How does this government department help individual prospective adoptive parents?
Answers general questions about either private or public adoption, although a local public agency may be more helpful with respect to procedural questions.

* * *

Adoptions by Residents of Other Provinces

All provinces, except Quebec, allow residents of other provinces to privately adopt a child born in the province. When such an adoption is to occur, the laws of the province where the child is born and the province where the prospective adoptive parents live must be considered. Adoption professionals in the two provinces will need to work together to determine whose rules must be followed during each segment of the process. The following will, however, give you a basic understanding of the concerns.

Although two provinces are involved, only one province will issue the adoption order completing the adoption. All provinces are willing to issue an order to prospective adoptive parents living in the province, no matter where the child is born. Some provinces are also willing to issue the order when the child to be adopted is born in the province, but the prospective adoptive parents live in another province. When a child is born in these provinces, the prospective adoptive parents may choose where to apply for the adoption order. The decision should be made after examining the relative advantages of the two alternatives.

Generally, most of the rules and procedures that must be followed are determined by the province issuing the adoption order. However, there are certain areas where a province will demand compliance even if the adoption order is to be issued by another province.

First, some provinces have special notification or approval requirements when a non-resident wants to remove a child born in the province for the purposes of adoption. In addition, it is not always easy to determine which province's procedures and time periods for signing and withdrawing the consent to adoption will apply.

The consent is usually signed in the province where the child is born. Some provinces recognize consents signed under other provinces' rules; others demand their consent rules be followed. It is possible to have conflicting requirements that must be worked out.

Finally, a province will not allow a non-resident to break its searching rules, even if the adoption order is to be issued elsewhere. For example, searching for a birth mother through advertising is legal in Ontario and illegal in New Brunswick. Ontario residents may not advertise in New Brunswick, even though they intend to obtain the adoption order in Ontario.

Confused? I would be surprised if you were not. This is a confusing area of adoption law; you need the assistance of an adoption professional.

However, if you have a lead in another province, do not be discouraged from pursuing it. As previously mentioned, my son was born in a different province than where we live. Complications can generally be worked out.

If you would like to consider the rules you will probably need to follow, look at the preceding discussion, the following charts and the provincial summaries. Keep in mind that you have only been given the basic considerations; your understanding must be confirmed with your adoption professional before you act upon it.

May a resident of another province privately adopt a child born in _____? If yes, what special notification or approvals are required?

ALBERTA	Yes.

B.C.	Yes.

MANITOBA	Yes. Prior approval of the birth parents' local public agency is required. Approval is generally given once it is determined that the adoption can be legally completed in the prospective adoptive parents' province.

NEW BRUNSWICK	Yes. Prospective adoptive and birth parents must give notice to the Minister of the Department of Health and Community Services within 15 days after placement.

NEWFOUNDLAND	Yes. A birth parent of the child must remove the child from the province.

NORTHWEST TERRITORIES	Yes.

NOVA SCOTIA	Yes. A birth parent of the child must remove the child from the province. Otherwise, an exit permit from the Minister of Community Services is required. An exit permit is generally not issued unless there is no suitable adoption home available in the province.

ONTARIO

Yes. Prior approval of the Director of the Ministry of Community and Social Services is required. Approval is generally given if (i) the laws of both Ontario and the province where the prospective adoptive parents live have been met, and (ii) the child remains in Ontario until the consent withdrawal period has expired. The prospective adoptive parents must work with an Ontario licensee approved to work in their province.

P.E.I.

Yes. Prior approval of the Director of Child Welfare is required. The Director considers: wishes of the birth parents, number of children available for placement relative to availability of prospective adoptive parents in P.E.I., risk of commercial influence, lack of clear and reliable planning, indication of misrepresentation or improper motive, any other factor that may pose a risk to best interests of the child. Approval is given if placement appears satisfactory in terms of criteria and specific P.E.I. procedural requirements are met.

QUEBEC

No.

SASKATCHEWAN

Yes. At least thirty days before removing the child from Saskatchewan, the person removing the child must give the Director of Family and Youth Services written notice of the removal. The Director will ensure that the prospective adoptive parents' province is regulating the adoption.

YUKON

Yes.

*If a resident of another province may privately adopt a child born in
_____, may the non-resident apply for an
adoption order in _____?*

ALBERTA	No.
B.C.	No.
MANITOBA	No.
NEW BRUNSWICK	Generally, no.
NEWFOUNDLAND	Generally, no.
N.W.T.	Yes.
NOVA SCOTIA	Yes.
ONTARIO	No.
P.E.I.	Yes.
QUEBEC	N/A.
SASKATCHEWAN	Generally, no.
YUKON	No.

Endnotes

[1] Generally, children are considered to have special needs if they are physically, emotionally or cognitively challenged; older; part of a sibling group;
of racial or ethnic minority status; or have a history that suggests future
problems. For a more detailed discussion, see Chapter 5.

[2] Licensee adoptions are generally full-service adoptions provided by an
agency or individual licensed by provincial authorities. In an independent
or identified adoption, prospective adoptive parents search for and find
their child themselves, using adoption professionals when necessary. For
more information, see Chapter 3.

[3] No province allows birth parents to be paid in relation to the adoption
of their birth child. This is to prevent any suggestion that the birth parents were induced to place their child with the prospective adoptive parents by a payment or gift.

The provinces also control, in varying degrees, other types of payments
made by the prospective adoptive parents. Generally, no one can be paid
for bringing birth and adoptive parents together. This restriction even
applies to paying a lawyer, since generally only the payment of proper
or reasonable legal fees are permitted and a payment to create a match
would not be so considered.

Making payments that are prohibited is generally an offence punishable by a fine. However, such illegal payments could also be enough to prevent the issuance of the adoption order. Often, a listing of the expenses paid by the prospective adoptive parents throughout the adoption process must be supplied to the court issuing the adoption order. Due to the possible severe consequences of making illegal payments, the phrasing used in the relevant law (confusing as it may be) has been repeated in the provincial summaries.

4 Most provinces state the factors that must be considered when deciding whether the birth father must consent to the adoption. In the past, unmarried birth fathers have generally been ignored. They are starting to become more vocal in their demand for fair treatment. It is therefore advisable, whenever possible, to obtain the birth father's consent, even if it does not appear to be required. Given the importance of the decision to require the birth father to consent, the phrasing used in the relevant law has been repeated in the provincial summaries.

It is possible to complete an adoption without the consent of either birth parent. Each province stipulates circumstances when a judge will dispense with the consent. Since the use of these provisions in a private adoption is rare, they have not been set out in the provincial summaries.

5 An affidavit contains written statements made under oath. Often affidavits as well as consents, notifications and applications are required to be in a specific format.

6 In looking at what is in the *best interests of a child*, a court will "choose the course which will best provide for the healthy growth, development and education of the child so that he will be equipped to face the problems of life as a mature adult." (Supreme Court of Canada in *King v. Low*, [1985] 1 S.C.R. 87, 101.)

7 Often a licensee or adoption professional prepares and files the required notices and applications for the prospective adoptive parents.

8 Guardians have the authority to, for example, consent to the child receiving medical treatment or leaving Canada for a vacation.

9 The application or petition for an adoption order is generally accompanied by supporting material such as the child's registration of live birth, the prospective adoptive parents' marriage certificate, the consent to the adoption, affidavits of the birth parents and the witnesses, and all of the materials gathered or created during the adoption investigation.

chapter · · · · · · · · · · · · · · · · · 5

Looking at the Adoption Alternatives

Most of this book focuses on the adoption of a Canadian newborn who does not have special needs. There are other options that may be the right choice for you.

Special-needs Adoptions

A *special-needs adoption* involves the adoption of a child with—surprise—special needs. Like many adoption terms, the term *special-needs* does not have a precise meaning. Sometimes the term is used only to refer to children whose characteristics or circumstances make it difficult for them to secure an adoptive home—children who are in the care of government authorities and are *waiting* for an adoptive family. However, often the term has a wider meaning, encompassing children who require extra consideration but are not necessarily hard to place.

Children may be categorized as special-needs for a variety of reasons. There may have been known physical, emotional or intellectual disabilities. Their history may make it likely that they will develop problems as they get older. They may be older or part of a family group who should remain together. Since adopting across racial or ethnic lines has additional concerns, children who possess a racial or ethnic minority status are also considered to have special needs.

Given this definition, you should realize that a healthy newborn can still be considered to have special needs. The child may, for example, be of mixed race, have an older sibling or be considered *at risk* since his birth mother used drugs during the pregnancy.

A special-needs adoption is not for everyone. Parents cannot predict what problems their newborns, by birth or by adoption, will encounter as they grow. However, dealing with the future concerns of a child you love is different from choosing to love a child with existing concerns. It takes a special kind of person—not a super parent—but someone who can embrace the extra needs of their child.

Since you are considering adoption, you have the opportunity to examine your needs, desires and abilities with respect to the type of child you adopt. Just as your infertility caused you to determine why it was important for you to parent a child, you should explore the type of child you want to parent.

The choice may be obvious. You want to grow into parental responsibilities. You do not want your child to have a previous life history. You want your child to have the same racial background as you or your spouse. You want as *normal* a parenting experience as possible.

If the choice is not so obvious, investigate. You may discover that a special-needs adoption is exactly how you want to become a parent. Many adoptive parents do not start the adoption learning process knowing that they want to adopt a child with special needs. Instead, they grow into the decision as they learn more about the children, themselves and their options.

Start your inquiry by reading books such as *Adopting the Older Child*[1] by Claudia Jewett, *Adopting Children with Special-needs: A Sequel*[2] edited by Linda Dunn or any other publication of the North American Council on Adoptable Children (NACAC). NACAC is a nonprofit organization committed to meeting the needs of children waiting for adoptive families in the U.S. and Canada (see Appendix I for contact information).

Ask a local adoptive parents support group or adoption organization (see Appendix I) to point you towards the special-needs adoption resources in your community. See if they can arrange for you to talk to adoptive parents who have been just where you are now.

If you are considering the adoption of a child of a different race or ethnicity, make sure you read the next section on International Adoptions. Since adopting across racial and ethnic lines is a factor in many international adoptions, the section addresses some of the additional concerns.

Working with your local public agency is a viable option in a special-needs adoption. Remember, most of the children in the care of the public agencies have special needs and are waiting for adoptive families. However, also keep in mind that not all special-needs children are hard to place. The characteristics of children who are waiting for families changes depending on the community.

Once you have relayed serious interest in adopting a special-needs child to your local public agency, your homestudy should be done relatively quickly. Depending on the type(s) of special-needs you are interested in, the next step is either a discussion about a particular child or learning about the waiting children.

Several different methods are used by the provinces to introduce the waiting children. There may be books of profiles and photos you may review. Adoption newsletters or bulletins, the daily newspaper or television shows may be used to present profiles. You may be invited to a meeting where video or slide displays are used. Perhaps you, like many adoptive parents, will fall in love with a picture of your future child.

International Adoptions

An *international* or *intercountry adoption* occurs when the prospective adoptive parents and the child to be adopted live in different countries. International adoption has been used by many Canadians to create their families.

Discussions about international adoption could easily fill a separate book. This section introduces some additional issues that must be considered when the adoption is an international one. You are then presented with a general description of the process. Finally, the differences between international and domestic adoptions are highlighted. If the provided information piques your interest, further research will be necessary to ensure that you are comfortable with the issues and that you understand how to proceed.

Issues Requiring Attention

Characteristics of the Children

Three characteristics of children who are adopted internationally—health, racial and ethnic background—require extra reflection. Internationally adopted children are generally not placed with the adoptive parents until they are at least several months old. Often their prenatal and early months have been less than ideal. They may have experienced poor maternal nutrition during pregnancy, inadequate infant nourishment, no pre- or post-partum medical care, several care givers, institutional care, sensory deprivation or physical and emotional abuse.

Medical conditions caused by these factors sometimes go undetected in initial physical examinations. As well, the existence of these factors places a child at risk for the development of cognitive, emotional or behavioural disabilities.[3] These concerns are a reality you must consider.

Adopting a child with a different ethnic or cultural background from the adoptive parents is called a *transethnic adoption*. Similarly, if a child's racial background is different, the adoption is *transracial*. Almost all international adoptions are transethnic; many are also transracial.

Since the 1970s, there has been much debate in the United States on whether a transracial adoption is in the best interests of the child. Transracial adoptions generally involve children possessing a racial minority status being adopted by parents of a non-minority status. Some claim that these children not only lose their racial identity, but are left unprepared to deal with today's often racist society.

These concerns have caused many public agencies and some private adoption professionals in the United States to only consider placing a child with adoptive families of the same race or to wait a certain length of time before agreeing to a transracial adoption. While Canadian professionals recognize these concerns, a child's need for a permanent home appears to have a higher priority. Generally, if a same race home cannot be found for a particular child, a transracial adoption will immediately be considered.

As international adoption increased in popularity, a similar worry about crossing ethnic lines surfaced. Do transethnic adoptions weaken the ethnic identity of the children? Are the children able to handle any discrimination they encounter?

Both critics and advocates of international adoption quote the same studies as support for their positions.[4] These studies have generally found that transracially or transethnically adopted children experience discrimination and have a weak racial or ethnic identity. However, the studies conclude that the children adjust well; the children assess their family relationships positively and have good self-esteem.

Families created by transracial and transethnic adoptions argue that these seemingly contradictory findings reflect a rigid definition of identity. They acknowledge that their children's identity may be different from those raised in a single ethnic or race home, but stress that it need not be weaker. By learning about and participating in the culture of their children's background, a feeling of belonging and a sense of pride in that background can be instilled in the children. Yet the children also have the unique opportunity to feel at home among those of a different race or ethnicity.

Encountering prejudice in Canada is unfortunately not as unique as we would like to think. The 1994 study *Intercountry Adoption in*

Canada found that "visible minority children who are adopted from out-of-country are highly likely to experience some form of discrimination or racism in Canada."[5]

The multiracial or multiethnic family must develop strategies to cope with discrimination. Note that the whole family and not just the adoptee must be prepared. When a child of a minority race or ethnicity is adopted, a minority family is created. The child will grow, marry and have kids—forever changing the family.

What does all this mean? Are internationally adopted children destined to have problems? No. Most do well in their new country, becoming happy and healthy adults. However, love and patience are not always enough.

The Ethics

International adoption has never been more popular among prospective adoptive parents and more controversial within the general public. Why?

Before the 1970s, there were North American infants without special needs readily available for adoption. North Americans adopting children from less developed countries did so mainly out of concern for the well-being of those children.

During the 1970s, increased support for single mothers and increased availability of abortion and birth control began to cause the number of infants available for adoption to decline. Since these factors are generally not present in less-developed countries, the number of adoptable infants in those countries did not similarly decline. Therefore, many infertile North Americans began looking to these less-developed countries to fulfil their desire to parent.

As eager and often naive North Americans looked for their children, some abuses occurred. We have heard all about them—the selling and buying of children, the corrupt officials and intermediaries who demand payment.

Everyone agrees that abuses should not be tolerated. No one should be exploited—the children, the birth families or the adoptive families. Steps must be taken to ensure that the best interests of the children are being served. However, this concern must be kept in perspective. Too often, one only hears about the few disasters and not about the thousands of successes.

The shift from altruism to parenting as the main motivational factor for international adoption also caused some to argue against not the abuses but international adoption itself. Critics maintain that international adoption is simply one more way in which the rich exploit the poor—taking their children. They contend that the children suffer because, as discussed above, their ethnic and racial identities are weakened and the less-developed country suffers because its resources, its children, are being taken away. Not only are the children being taken away today but forever, the critics stress, since the pressure is off the country and the rest of the world to help make changes that would improve the lives of the future children.

Generally, the response to these claims is that new, different and healthy multiracial and multicultural families are being created. International adoptions not only meet the needs of adoptive parents but of children who cannot be cared for by their birth parents; children whose very lives may be in danger. These children in distress should not suffer because their country is embarrassed by its inability to provide for them. Adopting the children does not relieve the pressure for social change but rather heightens the public's awareness of the children and their country's plight.

To adopt internationally, you must feel comfortable with the ethics of international adoption in general and the particular circumstances of your adoption. You, and more important, your child, will suffer from any doubts.

The Process

The international adoption process may seem overwhelming. This is not surprising since the process must reflect the laws of the province where the adoptive parents live, Canadian immigration laws and any relevant laws in the country where the child to be adopted lives.

Public Adoptions

As with domestic adoptions, there are public and private international adoptions. A public international adoption is an adoption facilitated by the National Adoption Desk (the "Desk") in Ottawa.

The Desk was established by the federal Department of National Health and Welfare in 1975. It acts as an international adoption consultant and coordinator. The Desk obtains information on the adoption laws and policies of other countries. The details are then relayed to the provincial governments to help them advise prospective adoptive parents.

The Desk also develops programs with foreign countries. A country's program consists of various policies and procedures to help Canadians who wish to adopt children from that country. All provinces, except Quebec, allow their residents to use some or all of the Desk programs.

The programs differ from country to country. How a province allows its residents to utilize those programs also varies. Generally, after spending time learning about the countries with an available program, prospective adoptive parents pick one or two countries. They apply to the countries through their provincial government department responsible for adoptions. The province then forwards the application to the Desk, which forwards it to the government or agent of each foreign country. The Desk works with the province and the foreign country or its agent to help arrange the adoption and ensure that all requirements are met.

The application must include an international homestudy report as well as any documents required by the particular program country. The documents usually include such items as birth and marriage certificates, police checks, letters of reference, financial statements, and medical reports. Generally, they must be notarized; sometimes, they must be translated into the language of the foreign country.

After anywhere from several months to several years, the foreign government or its agent will match the prospective adoptive parents with a child. Information about the child is then presented to the prospective adoptive parents. If they wish to proceed with the adoption of that child, the necessary procedures to complete the adoption must then be followed.

The steps that must be taken vary depending on which foreign country and which province is involved and where the adoption is to be completed. Most foreign countries require the adoption of a child living in the country to be completed (an adoption order issued) by a court in that country. The child is then brought into Canada as the legal child of the adoptive parents. Many of the adoption procedural requirements are therefore determined by and completed in the foreign country. The provincial government may have little involvement.

With other countries, the prospective adoptive parents take the child out of the country, completing the adoption in the province where they live. In these circumstances, the procedures to complete the adoption depend largely on the laws of the prospective adoptive parents' province. However, the foreign country will also have requirements to meet.

Regardless of where the adoption is to be completed, the child's entrance into Canada must be sponsored. To sponsor a child, prospective adoptive parents must first complete an *Undertaking of Assistance* form obtained from their local Canada Employment and Immigration office. After the completed form is returned, the Immigration office contacts the provincial department responsible for adoptions and asks for a letter of no-objection to the proposed adoption.

The provincial letter and sponsorship form are sent to the Canadian Consulate or Embassy closest to the child's place of birth. An immigrant visa allowing the child to enter Canada is issued after the Consulate or Embassy is satisfied that Canadian immigration requirements (medical fitness, passport, etc.) have been met. When visa requirements cannot be met, a *Minister's permit* may be issued to allow the child to enter Canada. There are then additional steps that must be taken in Canada in order for the child to become a landed immigrant.

The travel logistics of the adoption also changes depending on the foreign country. The prospective adoptive parents may be able to choose between travelling to the country to pick up their child and having the child escorted to Canada by approved representatives, or the decision may be mandated. In any event, the child will require a passport and, in some countries, an exit visa to leave the foreign country.

Many countries' programs request post-adoption reporting. The requirements continue for varying lengths of time, sometimes persisting until the child is an adult.

Private Adoptions

Canada has public adoption programs with a small number of countries. Canadians must privately adopt a child from any other country. In addition, some countries that have programs allow Canadians to choose whether to adopt through the Desk or privately.

Canadians who want to privately adopt a child born in a foreign country generally have two options. They may work with a Canadian or American adoption professional that has connections in the foreign country or go directly to the foreign country and work with adoption professionals there. The adoption professional may be an agency or other type of organization or a lawyer or other category of individual. Some provinces do, however, place restrictions on how and through whom their residents may internationally adopt.

In a private international adoption, the prospective adoptive parents and their adoption professional must find the child and arrange for the completion of all procedural requirements themselves. The division of the required work depends on what the professional is willing to do and what the prospective adoptive parents want done. Usually, the more the professionals are asked to do, the more they are paid. However, the cost, type and quality of assistance varies greatly. It is imperative that prospective adoptive parents research before hiring. The discussion in Chapter 6 provides a starting point.

The basic structure of a private international adoption is the same as a public international adoption. Each foreign country has its own requirements and procedures. The country will specify where the adoption must be completed. Immigration Canada must issue a visa to allow entrance into Canada. Provincial government involvement varies among the provinces. If the adoption is to be completed in the foreign country, many provinces have little interest in the proceedings.

The Differences between Public and Private International Adoptions

The differences between an international adoption processed through the Desk and one processed privately are akin to those between a domestic public and private adoption. Everything flows from the fact that in a private adoption the prospective adoptive parents and their adoption professional find the child and arrange for the completion of the adoption themselves.

Generally, adopting through the Desk takes longer but is considerably cheaper. Most of the Desk programs have waiting periods of several years, although there are new programs that are promising quicker results. However, those waiting periods do not begin to run until all the documentation has been received by the foreign country. Remember, the documentation must go through the responsible provincial government department and the Desk before being forwarded to the foreign country. All this time can be avoided by going the private route.

In a public international adoption, costs could be as little as several thousand dollars, while it is not unheard of to incur expenses of $20,000 or more in completing a private international adoption. The drastic difference can easily be explained. The adoption professionals involved in private international adoption are interested in making a profit. Not only are the Canadian and foreign governments not interested in profit, most administrative costs in processing the adoption are not passed on to the prospective adoptive parents. As with most public programs, all taxpayers rather than individual users of the program pay such costs.

Adopting privately allows prospective adoptive parents to hire adoption professionals of their choosing rather than work with assigned government personnel. In addition, depending on the foreign country and the adoption professional involved, the prospective adoptive parents may have the ability to influence the outcome of the adoption by using their own energy and initiative. However, generally they cannot be considered to have control of the process. Too often, a foreign government changes the procedures or requirements in the middle of an adoption, requiring the prospective adoptive parents to regroup and sometimes to move on to another country.

Using the Desk makes partners of all of the governments involved. The threat of changes in the rules during a particular adoption is therefore reduced. Some may also feel more comfortable with respect to the ethical issues discussed above.

A private adoption may eliminate the need for an international homestudy and post-adoption reporting. This is especially important in the provinces where prospective adoptive parents are not allowed to hire, or have difficulty finding, adoption professionals to help meet these requirements.

The Hague Convention

There is one more factor about international adoption procedures that should be addressed. In May of 1993, the text of the *Hague Convention on Intercountry Adoption*[6] was finalized. The Convention is a treaty that will cover adoptions between countries that become parties to the Convention. Its objective is to establish consistent adoption procedures that (i) ensure the best interests of the child is the paramount consideration in an adoption, and (ii) secure recognition of the adoption among treaty countries.

Delegates from approximately sixty-five countries attended the Convention discussions. Those delegates have now taken the Convention back to their countries. Each country must decide whether it will become a party to the Convention by signing and ratifying it. To ratify the Convention, a country must incorporate the required procedures into its adoption laws. This means that in order for Canada to ratify the Convention each province will need to amend its adoption laws. At that time, international procedures, as well as domestic procedures, may change considerably. We can only hope that procedures intended to prevent abuses will not be so cumbersome that they prevent adoptions.

How Domestic Adoptions Differ

The major differences between an international and a domestic adoption are the issues discussed above: the health, race and ethnicity of the children and the ethical considerations. Other distinctions exist.

A private domestic adoption generally involves the adoption of a newborn. A child adopted internationally is rarely under several months old.

The cost of a private or public international adoption can be substantially greater than its domestic counterpart. In addition, travelling to the foreign country is often required. Some consider the travel an adventure; it gives them time to learn about their children's country and to bond away from well-meaning family and friends. However, many find it very stressful and inconvenient—time away from work, poor living conditions, unknown language and customs, little or no notice of travel date and constant delays.

Any travel that might be required in a domestic adoption will probably be shorter and much easier—no language barrier, familiar living conditions, rare surprises. If you run into difficulties, help is easily available.

The circumstances of many international adoptions do not allow the adoptive family to have a relationship with the birth parents, although some countries require that the birth parents maintain the right to contact the child. Prospective adoptive parents may initially feel relieved by this lack of contact, especially since it generally means that there are no birth parents around to change their minds and decide to parent as may happen in a domestic adoption. However, as previously discussed, some contact, or at least some knowledge, of the birth parents is something that many adopted children will want and cherish later in life.

In addition, although birth parents changing their minds is often not a major concern in an international adoption, there are still risks. A country may suddenly decide to forbid any adoptions by foreigners. An official may suddenly decide that a child assigned to particular prospective adoptive parents should go to others. Unfortunately, there is rarely someone who will listen to the resulting cries.

Once you look past the Canadian borders, there are many children available for adoption. This is the definitive advantage in deciding to adopt internationally. Unfortunately, the availability of more children does not always materialize into a quicker adoption experience. Complicated and ever-changing procedures as well as language barriers slow down many international adoptions.

Additional Research

As with almost anything, the best resources are those who preceded you down the road. Local adoption organizations or adoptive parents support groups should be able to put you in touch with families who have used international adoption to create those families. Talk to them about their experiences and your concerns.

To learn more about the issues glance at Anne Westhues' and Joyce Cohen's 1994 study *Intercountry Adoption in Canada* and some of the other studies it reviews. Read Elizabeth Bartholet's *Family Bonds: Adoption & The Politics of Parenting*.[7] Intertwined in her adoption story are thought-provoking critiques of many of society's adoption policies. There is also Cheri Register's terrific book *Are Those Kids Yours?: American Families with Children Adopted from Other Countries*.[8]

For help with the international adoption process, contact your provincial government department responsible for adoptions (see Chapter 4). Ask for information on adopting internationally, both through a National Adoption Desk program and privately.

Subscribe to the fantastic Toronto newsletter *Adoption Helper* (see Appendix I). In addition to country updates that keep you abreast of the changing adoption process abroad, several times a year it provides personal adoption stories, a summary of adoption news around the country and articles on current adoption issues. You should also read John Bowen's *A Canadian Guide to International Adoptions.* Although the details about the foreign countries may be out-of-date (it doesn't take long!), it contains helpful information.

Read the next section, "Looking Across the American Border." Many Canadians have successfully used American adoption professionals to adopt internationally. Since choosing an adoption professional will be one of the most important decisions you make, you may also want to glance at the relevant discussions in Chapter 6.

Looking Across the American Border

Given the proximity of the U.S. and the similarity of the American and Canadian cultures, looking across the border is a viable adoption alternative for most Canadians. In many ways, the Canadian and American adoption experiences are similar. Like the provinces, each state has its own laws. The same questions answered for each province in Chapter 4 could be used to describe the legal situation for each state. There are, however, a few major differences that should be kept in mind.

All of the states have public agencies and licensees that provide full-service private adoptions. Since only agencies are licensed, licensees are called *licensed private agencies* or simply *private agencies.* There may be as few as a handful or as many as one hundred private agencies in any one state. Public and private agencies are often lumped together as *agencies.*

The term *private adoption* is used interchangeably with the term *independent adoption.* It is only used with respect to non-agency adoptions; an adoption processed through a private agency is not considered a type of private adoption.

To adopt a child through an agency, a Canadian must find an agency that is willing and legally able to work with Canadians. The Canadian applies to the agency and, if accepted, follows the agency's instructions until they are matched with a child and the adoption is completed.

As in Canada, most of the adoptions facilitated by a public agency are special-needs adoptions. Private agencies vary greatly in policies and services. They may have a particular focus—special-needs adoptions, international adoptions, adoptions involving minority children or adoptive families. Some will only assist members of a particular religious denomination or residents of a specific geographical area. Others are only licensed to conduct homestudies and counselling; another agency must be used to place the child in the prospective adoptive parents' home. They may have age, marital status, family size and income requirements.

A licence does not guarantee quality. In many states, an agency need only have the required staffing and organization to obtain a licence.

An agency is generally not the best way for a Canadian to adopt an American newborn without special needs. Since there are many Americans who want to adopt such a child, the waiting lists are long, the requirements strict and the costs high. There are, however, private agencies willing to work with Canadians who want to pursue a special-needs or international adoption.

Included in the special-needs category are black or mixed-race healthy newborns. Generally, there are not enough interested American prospective adoptive parents, possibly because of the strong opposition to transracial adoptions in the black community.

Independent adoption has become big business in the U.S. There are many lawyers and *facilitators* willing to help prospective adoptive parents who want to adopt a child born in or out of America. Some of these adoption professionals will work with Canadians.

Most lawyers will provide legal assistance to prospective adoptive parents who find their own birth parents. Some lawyers give the necessary legal assistance and find the birth parents.

Facilitators are generally not lawyers or licensed agencies; they cannot legally complete the adoption. Many facilitators are paid a great deal of money to do only one thing—find prospective adoptive parents a baby. They or you must then hire a lawyer to finalize the adoption. Paying a facilitator is illegal in most provinces and many states. However, they do exist in the U.S. and there are Canadians who have successfully adopted through them.

Using a facilitator is controversial. Some feel that they provide an essential service; others feel that using them is akin to buying a baby.

Even without the use of a facilitator, an American independent adoption is generally more expensive than its Canadian counterpart. In Canada and the U.S., it is usually illegal for the prospective adoptive parents to make any type of direct or indirect payment to the birth parents, unless the payment is for specific legally approved types of expenses incurred by the birth parents. Generally in Canada, only adoption legal and counselling expenses may be reimbursed by the prospective adoptive parents. Since there is no government medical plan in the U.S., most states allow uninsured pregnancy medical expenses to be covered by the prospective adoptive parents. Some states also permit the reimbursement of the birth mother's living expenses during the pregnancy.

What does all this mean? A Canadian may generally look across the American border to (i) adopt a special-needs American child through an American private agency, (ii) independently adopt an American child using a lawyer or facilitator, or (iii) adopt a child from a third country with the help of an American private agency or adoption professional.

Remember that adopting a child from the U.S. or a third country is still an international adoption. The laws of the state or third country where the child is born, the province where the prospective adoptive parents live and Canada Immigration determine the procedures that must be followed to complete the adoption. As well, some of the international adoption discussion above may be applicable.

There are several good books that can provide more details about the American adoption experience. If you are interested in pursuing an American adoption, you may want to glance at, for example, Lois Gilman's *The Adoption Resource Book*,[9] Cynthia Martin's *Beating the Adoption Game*[10] or Randall B. Hicks' *Adopting in America*.[11] Nancy Thalia Reynolds' *Adopting Your Child*[12] has a chapter specifically for Canadians considering adopting in or through the United States. You may also want to use the information provided in Chapter 6 to help you locate an American private agency or adoption professional.

Endnotes

[1] Jewett, Claudia. *Adopting the Older Child*. Harvard: Harvard Common Press, 1978.

[2] Dunn, Linda (editor). *Adopting Children with Special Needs: A Sequel*. Washington: North American Council on Adoptable Children, 1983.

[3] Verhulst, F.C. and M. Althaus and H. Verluis-den Bieman. Damaging backgrounds: Later adjustment of international adoptees. *Journal of the American Academy of Child and Adolescent Psychiatry, 31*, 1992, 518-524.

[4] For a good review of the literature, see *Intercountry Adoption in Canada*, 11-32.

[5] *Intercountry Adoption in Canada*, 173.

[6] The formal title is *Convention on Protection of Children and Co-operation in Respect of Intercountry Adoption*.

[7] Bartholet, Elizabeth. *Family Bonds: Adoption & The Politics of Parenting*. New York: Houghton Mifflin, 1993.

[8] Register, Cheri. *Are Those Kids Yours?: American Families with Children Adopted from Other Countries*. New York: The Free Press, A Division of Macmillan, Inc., 1991.

[9] Gilman, Lois. *The Adoption Resource Book*. New York: HarperPerennial, 1984, 1987, 1992.

[10] Martin, Cynthia D. *Beating the Adoption Game*. Orlando: Harvest Brace Jovanovich, 1988.

[11] Hicks, Randall B. *Adopting in America*. Sun City, California: WordSlinger Press, 1993.

[12] Reynolds, Nancy Thalia. *Adopting Your Child*. Vancouver: Self-Counsel Press, 1993.

chapter •••••••••••••••••• **6**

Planning Your Adoption

You are overwhelmed. You have just finished reading the first five chapters and are confused. What are you supposed to do with all that information? How do you get started on your way?

You get started by using that information to create an adoption plan. You ensure a smooth journey by hiring experienced adoption professionals to help.

Creating an Adoption Plan

An adoption plan is simply a timetable with various courses of action. It need not be a detailed chart, but rather a strategy that enables you to feel confident that you are doing everything you can to reach your parenting goal.

Your adoption plan should attempt to match your desires, resources and limitations with the options available to you. To do this, you must first understand your adoption alternatives. Self-examination and frank discussions between you, your spouse and your extended family will then be necessary.

Begin by rereading the general description of the methods available to adopt a Canadian newborn set out in Chapter 3. Then examine the specific adoption procedures for your province set out in Chapter 4. Pay particular attention to the types of private adoption available and to the type of search methods you may use to search for your child.

When considering the self-directed adoption of a Canadian newborn, whether an independent or an identified adoption, keep in mind that most of the adoption process will probably be spent searching for your child. More specifically, you will be searching for a pregnant woman considering adoption for her unborn child—the birth mother of your child. There are three basic search methods: networking, advertising and mailings. Each of these search methods is described in detail in Part II. After you realize which methods your province permits, you may want to skim the relevant chapters so that you have an idea how your time would be spent.

If there are licensees or other adoption professionals offering full-service adoptions in your province, check out these options. Use the information set out in the next section to contact and question the professionals.

Once you understand what is involved in adopting a newborn in your province, expand your boundaries. Consider adopting a child born in another province. Looking across provincial borders is discussed in Chapter 3, and which borders you may cross is set out in Chapter 4.

If a special-needs or international adoption has your interest, reread Chapter 5. Use the suggested resources to complete your understanding of the requirements, advantages and disadvantages.

In other words, you are not quite ready to begin. First, you must prepare. Use the information provided in Part I of this book and the additional resources set out in Chapter 2 to figure out exactly what options you have. The time you spend learning is invaluable. It will lead you to your child with the minimum amount of heartache.

Do not become caught up in labels. Your province may not use the same terminology found in this book. For example, many provinces use the general term *private adoption* to refer to whatever type of private adoption is permitted by the province. Similarly, *full-service adoption* and *self-directed adoption* are descriptive labels, not terms you can use without an explanation.

As you learn more about the alternatives, some will become more attractive, others less. You are subconsciously matching your desires, resources and limitations to the attributes of the options.

In looking at your desires, make sure you determine the characteristics of the child you wish to adopt—health, age, race, ethnicity. Consider the desired relationship with the birth parents of your child. Assess the privacy and control you hope to maintain. Evaluate the emotional risks you feel capable of sustaining. Weigh the importance of a speedy process.

In evaluating your resources and limitations, examine the amount of time, energy and money you have available. Count any special advantage you may have. Do you know people who come in regular contact with pregnant women considering adoption for their unborn child? Is your sister a doctor, your brother a minister?

Once you feel confident about your understanding of the factors that should be considered, list the adoption alternatives in the order of preference. Provide an initial estimate of how long you will spend on a particular option before moving on to another. Pursuing more than one avenue may not be necessary. However, if an option is not giving fast enough results, the list will serve as a reminder that there is more that can be done.

As you learn more about your chosen routes, additional planning may be possible. For example, if you are pursuing an independent or identified adoption and all of the search methods may be used, you may want to immediately start networking and creating your mailing list. Advertising may be your backup if nothing happens for several months.

Certain options can be pursued simultaneously. Everyone should, for instance, contact their local public agency and complete the necessary steps to get on its waiting list, even if you are not interested in its main focus, special-needs adoptions. You have very little to lose—a small amount of time.

However, do not overburden your resources or your emotions. Evaluate each option; carefully ration your assets. Create a livable plan that will lead you to your child.

Hiring Adoption Professionals

No book can replace the need for experienced adoption professionals. You must hire professionals to legally complete the adoption and to counsel you and the birth parents.

Why Experienced Professionals Are Needed

In a full-service adoption, the required adoption professionals are often part of the service. Your only consideration is which full-service organization or individual to hire. In self-directed adoptions, there are circumstances when hiring a legal advisor or a counsellor seems an unnecessary expense or bother. Do not succumb to these feelings. If you have done your homework and the adoption process goes smoothly, the costs and trouble will be small; you may never know what obstacles have been avoided. If problems start to appear, you will be thankful for the support.

Adoption laws are complicated and can change quickly. There are detailed requirements that, if not timely and accurately completed, could hinder the legality of your child's adoption. The legal adoption of your child is too important to put at risk.

Counselling can help equip you for the adoption experience—both the mechanics of adopting a child and the realities of parenting that child. Education, support and assistance in making decisions are just some possible benefits.

Birth parents must understand all of their options. Once they decide adoption is the right alternative for them, they will need help in dealing with the adoption process and the fact that they will not be parenting their birth child.

Most birth parents grieve for their birth children. If they have not considered their options or are not prepared for the onslaught of emotions, they may regret their adoption decision. Therefore, birth parent counselling is advantageous to both the prospective adoptive and birth parents. It not only increases the well-being of the birth parents, it decreases the likelihood of the birth parents suddenly changing their minds and deciding to parent.

Depending on the type of adoption and the jurisdictions involved, various organizations or individuals—licensees, agencies, private practice lawyers, government lawyers—may legally complete the adoption. Similarly, licensees, agencies, social workers, counsellors or therapists may be available to help prospective adoptive and birth parents make and live with their adoption decisions. The types of adoption professionals are not important; making sure that they have experience is essential.

If you needed surgery, you would not hire a general practitioner or a dermatologist. Similarly, only use a professional who is experienced in adoptions. Do not ask the family friend who practices real estate law for help. There is no question he is sincere. However, he may not know, or understand the importance of, each step in the process.

Experienced adoption professionals often provide extra benefits. They may point you towards adoption resources in your community, spot potential problems before they occur or even pass on a potential birth parent lead.

Some jurisdictions allow a single professional to represent both the prospective adoptive parents and the birth parents. The theory is that the process need not be adversarial, since everyone has the child's best interests at heart. While this is true, prospective adoptive and birth parents often have additional separate concerns. Independent legal advice and counselling may assure the birth parents that their interests are being served. In addition, no one can then question whether the birth parents' consent to the adoption is fully informed, thereby eliminating a legal and moral concern.

Finding the Right Professionals for You

The best way to find any type of professional is through recommendations by former clients. Phoning up several professionals whose names you obtained from some list and asking questions is a distant second choice. How often has the nicest sounding workman turned out to be a dúd? Even when you have taken the time to listen to three different explanations of how the roof should be fixed, were you happy with your choice? Did he do a good job? Was he available when the water was pouring in?

This is not to say that asking questions is unhelpful. Just keep in mind that some poor professionals have great selling skills and vice versa. Compiling a list of recommended professionals and then using questions to find a fit should be your first choice.

Ask the adoptive parents you know, or met at the last adoptive parent support group, about their adoption professionals. Look in your local adoption newsletter for stories involving satisfied adoptive parents and their adoption professionals. If you are interested in international adoption and are willing to work with professionals who do not have an office in your community, glance at issues of the Toronto newsletter *Adoption Helper*. (See Appendices I and II for contact information.)

If you are unable to use an adoptive parent's recommendation or want more names, try obtaining a referral from someone else you trust. For example, lawyers may know a good adoption lawyer or know someone whom they trust to provide a referral. Similarly, doctors specializing in infertility, obstetrics or gynaecology may know reliable adoption counsellors or lawyers.

If these options do not generate names, compile your own list of adoption professionals working in your community or on your type of adoption. Then make sure you ask for the names of, and talk with, satisfied clients.

When using a required type of adoption professional, such as a licensee or an approved social worker, lists of the professionals are often available through the government department responsible for adoptions. (See your provincial summary in Chapter 4 for contact information.)

There are often provincial organizations that govern the particular profession in question. For instance, each province has a law society that oversees lawyers, many of which have referral services.

Once you have the name of one type of professional, you can ask to be referred to the other type. An adoption lawyer can give you the names of adoption counsellors, and counsellors the names of lawyers.

Look for advertisements in the yellow pages or adoption newsletters. Check out the author of any interesting adoption articles. If you are creative and persistent, you should obtain results.

If you are looking across the border, you will have no problem finding the names of lawyers or private agencies. Many books contain lists. See, for example, the previously mentioned *The Adoption Resource Book* or *Adopting in America*. The Adoptive Families of America (AFA) will send you an introductory booklet on adoption that includes an agency listing. AFA also has an adoption hot line that can provide referrals. Similarly, the National Adoption Information Clearinghouse (NAIC) maintains a data base of experts knowledgeable in various areas of adoption practice and will provide referrals. (See Appendix I for contact information for AFA and NAIC.)

When deciding which professional to hire, search until you find someone you can trust. You need to feel confident not only in her advice but that she will be there when you need her. Make sure you agree with her philosophy. Do you want to know every detail or would you prefer not to be aware of the daily disasters? Avoid anyone who believes in shortcuts. If you are being urged to misrepresent the facts in any way, look for a new advisor. Do not be shy to ask about fees or to compare.

While you always want the professionals you deal with to be the best at everything, this is not always possible. Decide what is a necessity, what would be helpful and what you will forgo. Keep in mind what you want them to do. If he is going to work with prospective birth parents, communication skills may be top priority. If you are the only one going to deal with him, you may not care that he appears brash.

Before you can decide what you want a professional to do for you, you must understand what they can and are willing to do. Ask them to explain the adoption process and their and your roles in that process. Do not be satisfied with a general statement that they will take care of the details. A discussion will not only help you understand the process, but will give you a sense of their knowledge, communication skills and attitude in dealing with their clients.

When deciding on the division of work between the professional and yourself, remember that even to the most conscientious and caring advisor, your adoption is still a job. It is your life. They cannot possibly put as much thought or effort into the adoption as you.

Time is a professional's only product. Do not expect to talk to professionals at length, without paying for that time. Be up front. If you want an hour of their time to see if you feel comfortable with them, ask what it will cost. You do not want to be surprised by an invoice several months later.

*   *   *

You are now ready to handle the details of your chosen adoption alternative. You understand the adoption world and what is expected of you. If you have chosen to pursue a Canadian independent or identified adoption, read on. The details necessary to find your child are provided in Part II and to complete the adoption, in Part III. Otherwise, you know what you need to do. Go to it.

Part II

The Search for Your Child

chapter · · · · · · · · · · · · · · · · · · 7

Painting Your Self-Portrait

"You sound so wonderful that my sister wants to know if you will adopt her."

A pregnant woman speaking to the prospective adoptive parents of her unborn child.

A self-portrait? Why, you are wondering, do you need a self-portrait to search for your child? You have probably talked about your *circumstances* with too many doctors and well-intentioned friends and relatives. Why do you need to expose yourself any further?

In an independent or identified adoption, the search for your child is actually a search for a pregnant woman who is considering adoption for her unborn child. You are looking for the woman who will eventually become the birth mother of your child. Your search consists of using various methods to contact birth mothers either directly or indirectly.

Often, an indirect contact will not be of help immediately. For instance, you contact a doctor and explain that you are trying to adopt a child. The doctor will probably not have a patient who is currently considering adoption but may have one in the future. Unless the doctor happens to be a close relative or friend, you must provide her with some means of remembering you when she does have such a patient.

Even if the doctor remembers your quest, what happens once she has such a patient? Similarly, what if you contact a birth mother directly through, for example, an advertisement? Remember, she must consent to the adoption—she must choose you. How do you convince her that you are the right choice?

You are now beginning to understand. This is where you need a self-portrait. It can be used to remind contacts of your search and to convince a birth mother to choose you and your spouse as the adoptive parents for her child.

Notice that we have been discussing a birth *mother* and not birth *parents*. What about the birth father? Unfortunately, many birth fathers are not involved in the adoption process; they disappear when they learn of the pregnancy. Since it is easy for them to pretend nothing has happened, many choose to do just that. Not all, but many.

Therefore, your search efforts will be directed towards finding a birth mother. If there is a birth father in the picture, he is then included in the discussions.

Creating a Birth Mother Letter

One form of self-portrait or résumé that has worked for many adoptive parents is a letter to a birth mother. A letter format allows the discussion to be personal and informal. Addressing the letter to a birth mother encourages prospective adoptive parents to focus on the birth mother's concerns.

Figures 1 and 2 are birth mother letters used by two couples in the search for their child. Both couples are now adoptive parents.

Before you begin to write your birth mother letter, read the two letters provided. They will give you an idea of the type of letter that has been successful in the past. Later you may want to study them in more detail, referring back to them as your letter begins to take shape.

Figure 1

Hello —

Our names are Daphne and Ed. We are writing this letter because we very much want to adopt a child.

We know that this is a difficult time for you. However, we hope that this letter will reassure you that should you decide to place your child for adoption, he or she would have a life filled with love and happiness. It may also help you to know that you would be bringing unbelievable joy into the lives of two other people.

Let us tell you a little bit about ourselves. We are very close. We spend almost all of our time together. Sometimes it seems like we know each other's thoughts and finish each other's sentences.

Ed is 33 years old and a little shy around people he does not know. He has a great sense of humour and is patient and loving. Daphne is also 33, outgoing, warm and makes friends easily. All of our friends tell us we will make wonderful parents.

We have always wanted a family. We picked out our children's names long before we were married. The nursery is already planned; a puppy already chosen as a pet. While our inability to have a baby has been a great disappointment, it has brought us even closer together and has made us realize just how much we want a child.

We are also very close to our immediate families. Daphne has two brothers; Ed has one brother and one sister. Since none of them have kids yet, our child will receive the undivided love and support of many aunts and uncles and will be "spoiled rotten" by four grandparents and one great-grandmother.

We are lucky in that we also have many friends and a large extended family living close by. "Get togethers" are frequent, noisy and a lot of fun. Our child will have many young cousins and friends' children (some of them also adopted) to play and get into trouble with.

Ed has both a law and a business degree and speaks French (in addition to English). He works with his dad in a family-owned marketing company. The company is very successful and provides us with financial security. As well, since Ed is his own boss, he will be able to take lots of time off to be with our family.

Daphne is a lawyer but has taken time off to pursue our number one priority — starting a family. She plans to be a full-time mother once we adopt a child.

We have a wonderful life together. We spend weekends at Ed's family cottage — swimming and boating in the summer, skiing in the winter, reading and relaxing all year. When we are in the city, we play tennis, see our friends, go to movies, and work in our garden. We can't wait to share all of this with our child!

We live in our own home in a wonderful neighbourhood filled with trees and close to parks and playgrounds. There are lots of kids around and excellent schools within walking distance.

We have talked a lot about our feelings and what we will tell our child. Our child will know how he or she came into our family and what a difficult decision his or her birth mother had to make. He or she will also know that our love could not be any greater if we were the child's birth parents.

It is difficult to describe our whole life in one short letter, but we hope that we have told you enough to show that we have a lot of love and a good life to give to a child. We would be honoured if you would consider us as adoptive parents for your baby.

If you would like to talk to us, please call us, collect, at (xxx) xxx-xxxx, or, if you prefer, ask your doctor to call for you.

We wish you all the best.

Daphne and Ed

Figure 2

Dear Birth Mother,

We know that you are facing a very difficult decision about your baby's future and that it will be based only on your wanting to make sure that the baby has all the opportunities you are unable to provide at this time in your life. My husband and I would like to offer you an alternative to think about.

Years of fertility tests and unsuccessful treatments have convinced us even more that we want to have a family. We both adore kids and can't imagine our future without them. We have thought about adoption a great deal and we feel very excited that it is the right thing for us to do.

If you are thinking about having your baby adopted we want to assure you that we will raise the baby in a warm and loving environment. We will tell our child that he or she was born to someone who loved him or her very much and wanted the very best for him or her. Adoption will be explained openly and honestly and, if you wish, we will share everything we know about his or her background.

We would like to tell you a little about ourselves so that you can feel confident that we will offer your baby a secure and loving future. We are a happy, caring couple in our 30's. We complement each other well and are each other's best friend. We have known each other for seven years and have been married for four years. Both of us are university graduates. My husband is a successful accountant and I am a purchasing agent. I am looking forward to staying home as a full-time mother when we start our family.

My husband is 6'1'', weighs 185 pounds, has brown hair and brown eyes and a bushy beard. He is a thoughtful, sociable man with a good sense of humour who is fun to be with. He likes all sports, especially swimming, scuba diving and skiing. I am 5'6'', weigh 120 pounds and I also have brown hair and brown eyes. I think of myself as warm, energetic and self-motivated. I like to spend my free time doing needle crafts, going to my exercise class and cooking. Together we like to go for bike rides, long walks, to travel and to entertain friends and family. Also, we both do volunteer work in our community.

We were both very lucky to have parents who provided a wonderful family life. They gave us tremendous encouragement and we too will offer our child all the support we can so that he or she can reach his or her full potential, in any area of interest.

Family relations are very important to us. Our child will have two sets of grandparents as well as aunts, uncles and young cousins who he or she will see often. Adoption is not new to our family. My brother's daughter was recently adopted and she was welcomed to our family with great warmth and love. She is very special to all of us.

We are very touched that you would consider entrusting your baby to us. You are doing a very unselfish thing in considering giving the most precious gift imaginable.

If you are considering us as adoptive parents, please ask your doctor to contact us. Of course you will not be under any obligation whatsoever.

Sincerely,

Hopeful Adoptive Parents

Identifying Yourself

You need to decide how much identifying information you are going to provide in the birth mother letter, before you start to write. Your style of writing may be different if you use names. You have four options. You can give no names, false names, actual first names or actual full names.

Using actual full names in a birth mother letter eliminates the possibility of a confidential adoption. You may have decided that you would like, or don't mind, exchanging identifying information with the birth mother of your child. However, you should keep in mind that a birth mother may want to remain anonymous. If you do not put such information in the letter, you can always decide to provide it later.

On the other hand, actual full names may make the letter seem more personal and will simplify the way in which the birth mother can contact you. Since your identity is no longer an issue, you can put your telephone number and address in the letter. In addition, you can give the birth mother the option of contacting an adoption professional, such as your social worker, lawyer or agency, since she can tell the adoption professional which prospective adoptive parents she wants to discuss.

Using only first names will keep the birth mother letter personal while lessening, although not eliminating, the identification concern. You can supply an unlisted telephone number. You may not, however, be able to provide the option of contacting an adoption professional, since a birth mother can only relay your first name.

It should be kept in mind that it is not necessary that there be any telephone numbers in the birth mother letter. The letter will generally be sent with a cover letter. The cover letter will contain identifying information and the recipient, for example, a doctor, will be asked to remove the cover letter before giving the birth mother letter to his patient. Chapter 10 contains further details on the cover letter.

Since you would like the news of your search spread as far as possible, it may, however, be preferable to have the means of contacting you in the birth mother letter itself. The birth mother letter can then be passed around without the possibility of losing a lead.

Using false first names will totally eliminate the identification concern, but will show a lack of trust if your actual names are later used by mistake. Using no names eliminates both concerns but may be considered less personal.

Whew! And you've yet to write a word! Don't worry. None of these issues, and those that will be raised in the next few pages, are crucial. Do not let them overwhelm you. They are pointed out so that you can have the benefit of someone else's thoughts while you write your letter. There is no right or wrong way to write the letter. You should consider the points raised, examine the birth mother letters provided in Figures 1 and 2, and then write your letter, the way you want it written.

Setting the Tone

As you sit down to write your birth mother letter, keep in mind the rationale behind its creation. You want to adopt a child—perhaps the child of the birth mother reading the letter. This thought should govern both the tone and content of the letter. You want her to get to know you, to know that if she places her child with you, that child will have a terrific life. The letter may be your only chance to convince the birth mother to choose you. It may be your only contact with that birth mother.

Remember your audience. Many birth mothers are teenagers. They are not, however, unintelligent. Do not talk down to them. Also, remember their predicament. They are not happy to be in this situation.

Your letter should open with something like *Hello, Hi, Dear Friend* or *Dear Birth Mother*. Some people think that *Dear Birth Mother* has a warmer feel than the other choices. Others think that the possibly unfamiliar term *birth mother* would be perceived unfavourably. Choose which sounds best to you.

The bulk of the letter should talk about you and your spouse. You and the birth mother are discussing something very personal. Involve her in your life. Let her feel like she knows you. Make her think that being a part of your family will be wonderful.

Describing Yourself

If you have decided to use names, you may write the letter using *we* to describe joint issues and you or your spouse's name to describe individual issues as was done in the letter contained in Figure 1. If you are not using names, the letter set out in Figure 2 provides one format idea. Both parties sign the letter, yet the wife is considered the writer, using *I* and *my husband* to describe individual issues. As previously discussed, some birth mothers are more comfortable with a woman as their contact.

List your personal characteristics. Are you sensitive, caring, tall, athletic? Describe your interests. Do you like to play a musical instrument, fix cars, climb mountains? Discuss your job. Consider issues such as financial security, free time, priorities, child care. Describe your home and your neighbourhood.

With respect to your age, you can ignore it, state it, or specify a range, such as *in my thirties*. You may want to consider whether a birth mother will think that you are *old*. Obviously, it depends on the age of the birth mother. A young birth mother may, on first reading, consider *old* anyone beyond their twenties. After she has received a little counselling about adoption, she will probably think that early thirties is good, mid to late thirties is okay, and forty or older is, well, old.

If you are over forty, do not let this statement depress you. Many birth mothers will think that your age is irrelevant. Many others will think that your age is an advantage—that it shows maturity. Just be aware of how your age may be perceived, when deciding how to treat it in your birth mother letter.

Explore you and your spouse's relationship and lives together. Is it close, loving, supportive? How did you meet, how long have you been together? Explain how you enjoy sharing the same interests or how your differing interests allow you both to grow.

Show how a child will fit into your life. Will your priorities change? Will your child have a stay-at-home parent? If you already have children, clarify how they will feel about the new addition to the family.

If you are not married, you may need to overcome a birth mother's bias towards having two parents for her child. Address this issue directly. Explain why you want to be a single parent and how you intend to make it work for both you and your child.

Talk about your family and friends. Will there be a lot of cousins to play with or will your child get the undivided attention of his grandparents, aunts and uncles. Do your friends have kids; are they close by? Does your family include a pet?

Try to use images that provide a picture of your life. If you love music, is your stereo always on? Have you picked out a name or a pet for your child? Do you have an ice rink or a swing waiting in your backyard?

Mentioning your religion is another issue that requires some thought. If your religion is a major part of your life, you will probably want to raise it with the birth mother. However, given the unfortunate reality of prejudice and ignorance, if you are not Catholic or a member of a mainstream Protestant denomination, you may wish to delay this discussion until after the birth mother has had a chance to get to know you.

If your religion is not a major part of your life, you should consider whether it is important enough to discuss. Bear in mind that the birth mother may learn of your religion through other sources without having received the benefit of your say.

If you choose to mention your religion, attempt to combat any ignorance by explaining how it enriches your life. Does it provide you with a strong sense of family or community? Are there traditions or special festivals and holidays that are celebrated together? Does your involvement give you a feeling of contentment?

Be assertive with respect to your abilities as parents. State that you know, or your friends tell you, that you will make good parents. Make sure to mention any special circumstances that show experience in dealing with children. Are you a godparent, an involved aunt or uncle, a teacher, a doctor, a nurse?

You may want to mention your child rearing theories. Will you stress education? Will encouragement be your focus?

Emphasize that you cannot physically have a child, that you are not simply choosing to adopt rather than give birth to a child. Let her know that your thinking about adoption is very clear. She must understand that you are very comfortable with adoption as a means of creating your family, that your love for your child will not be any less. Mention any adopted children in your circle of family and friends to stress that your child will not be alone, that adoption is accepted.

Remembering Your Audience

Do not forget about the birth mother's pain. Express your sympathy. You may want to suggest that it may make her feel better to know that her pain will bring someone else joy. Or you may want to let her know that you too have felt pain, as these adoptive parents decided to do:

We understand that this may be the most difficult time in your life. And while we can't fully understand what you're experiencing at this time, we have lived through a similar pain of our own.

My husband and I both adore children and have been trying to have a baby for many years. When I finally became pregnant, we were both thrilled. But tragically, our baby died in my seventh month of pregnancy and none of the doctors have been able to tell us why. The loss of our first child was devastating for both of us. Since that time I have been trying and trying to become pregnant again, but without any luck, even though we've seen all kinds of doctors.

Sharing such pain may help the birth mother feel a connection with you. It will certainly allow her to feel sympathy for you.

Similarly, express your understanding of the difficulty of the decision she is facing. Reassure her that you know, and that her child will know, that she wants what is best for her child. *Her* child, not yet *your* child—make sure this is recognized in the wording of your letter.

You may want to give her information about the adoption process. You may, for example, explain the advantages of a private adoption over a public adoption as outlined in Chapter 3.

Finally, make sure you tell her what you want her to do. You want her to consider you and your spouse as the adoptive parents for her child. You want her to contact you, either directly by calling a provided telephone number or indirectly through, for example, her doctor. Depending on what you have arranged with your adoption professionals, you may also give the birth mother the option of calling them.

Making Your Birth Mother Letter Unique

Now that you've written your birth mother letter, you may want to find a way to make it stand out from any other birth mother letters. For example, you can use high quality or coloured paper or include some art work.

You should also consider including a picture of yourself as part of your letter. In these circumstances, a picture is probably worth more than a thousand words. It makes you real in an unreal situation. One prospective adoptive couple thought so highly of the idea of giving a birth mother a picture, they made a video so that a birth mother could experience their lives.

A picture does have its negative side. A birth mother may not want to see what you look like—may not want you to be that real. You may also not want to be that real to the birth mother, if you have some reason to dislike the way you photograph. Maybe you've always looked unhappy in pictures or maybe you feel it will stress your age.

A picture also increases the possibility that a birth mother will discover your identity. In addition, it greatly increases the cost of your birth mother letter. You can, however, obtain a discount when ordering a large number of reprints of a photograph.

If you decide to include a picture, take the time to make sure it represents you. A formal picture suggests formal people—a fun picture, fun people. Is there a pet in your family? Does your neighbourhood have a great climbing tree? Consider including them in your picture.

Use a photograph small enough to fit into a standard business-size envelope. An oversized envelope would eliminate the need to fold your birth mother letter but it would also double the stamp costs.

Finally, do not sign the original letter. Make copies of the letter as needed and sign those copies. Signing each individual copy is extra work but an original signature is more personal than a photocopied one.

Your birth mother letter is now finished. Do you like it? Does it accurately describe you and your spouse—both as you are now and as you will be with your child? Does it make your eyes water? Is it a nice soft sales pitch? Yes, it is a sales pitch and there is nothing wrong with admitting it.

Like a job résumé, this birth mother letter is trying to sell you. You have taken your life and shown it at its best. This is expected. It is not wrong. But that being said, you must make sure that your letter is truthful as well as positive. Falsehoods will likely be discovered—either when the letter is read, because it does not quite ring true, or later, when the birth mother talks to you or your adoption professional.

Just be yourselves. Use the colours of your life to paint a positive self-portrait.

chapter • • • • • • • • • • • • • • • • • • 8

Getting and Staying Organized

Finally, the last preparation chapter. Just a few more ideas before
you begin to search for your child.

Preparing for the First Contact with the Birth Parents

You will soon learn how to spread the word about your search. If
you are successful, you will be contacted by the birth mother, or possibly the birth father, of your child.

The first contact could happen in a number of ways. My husband
and I received a Christmas card from the birth mother of our son.
You could be approached by one of the birth parents directly or by
someone helping them—a doctor, a neighbour. It could be over the
telephone, through the mail or by way of your adoption professional.
It does not matter how the first contact occurs; it only matters that
it happens and that you are prepared.

If the initial contact is through the mail or your adoption professional, you will have time before a response is needed. If an advisor
rather than a birth parent calls, emotions will not be as big a factor
in the conversation. As previously discussed, the birth father is often
not involved in the adoption arrangements. It therefore makes sense
to focus our discussion on answering a phone call from an unknown
prospective birth mother.

Before you answer that call, you must prepare. First, arrange for an unlisted telephone number and an answering machine or service. The answering machine is to prevent you from sitting at home waiting for your phone to ring. At least try to have a life while there is no requirement for a nine p.m. feeding (and a midnight feeding and a three a.m. feeding and . . .).

Distributing an unlisted number gives you and the birth mother the option of keeping the adoption confidential. Depending on your telephone company, there may be several ways to set up this temporary number.

You can always put a separate telephone line in your home. You may also have a cheaper option—assigning a second telephone number to your existing telephone line. This service, often called an *ident-a-call* or *smart-ring*, allows you to have a second telephone number that causes your telephone to ring with a distinct sound.

A third option is obtaining an *800 number*. An 800 number is also set up on an existing line and, if requested, may be unlisted. The advantage of an 800 number is that the caller does not need to worry about long-distance charges. The disadvantages are (i) you are not aware when the telephone rings that the call is an adoption call and (ii) it may be considered less personal—too much like a big business.

There are several reasons why you would like to know it is an adoption call. It gives you a few seconds to prepare. You can go to a designated quiet spot and pick up your notes. It allows you to decide who will and won't answer the phone. It also gives you a chance to pleasantly respond to an initial silence on the other end of the line: "Hi, this is Judy, are you calling about our desire to adopt?"

Yet eliminating long-distance charges with an 800 number is beneficial. You don't want anyone to hesitate because of the charges. With a regular phone number, you can tell everyone to call collect; but what if you are not home? One method is to set up the answering machine with a message stating: "If this is the operator, we accept all collect calls . . . [pause] . . . Hi, this is Judy. . . ." However, a problem may still exist if collect calls are handled by an automated system or if an operator disconnects before hearing your request.

The best method may be an 800 number with an ident-a-call feature—no long-distance charges to the caller and a warning that it is an adoption call—the wonders of technology.

As already mentioned, pick a quiet place to have the conversation and decide if you want someone in particular to answer the phone. We decided my office was the right spot and that I would answer the phone whenever I was home. We felt that a birth mother might feel more comfortable talking to a woman. In your quiet place, put a note pad, a pen and a list of relevant information and questions.

Our list began with the words *smile* and *relax* in big letters. It then listed a few simple introductory statements such as:

- Hi, I guess you're calling about our desire to adopt.
- I'm so glad you called.
- I'm really nervous—I bet you are too.
- This must be a difficult time for you.
- How are you feeling?
- My name is Judy, what's yours?
- Would you like to tell me about yourself or would you like to hear about me and my husband?
  [We are very close to each other and our families. We have lots of friends—most of them with kids. Our life together is terrific. Summers are spent swimming, boating and bicycling at a family cottage. In the winter we cross-country ski in our own backyard. All that is missing is a child to love . . .]

Finally, the information we wanted to give and receive was set out:

- When are you due?
- Is there anything you want to ask me? tell me?
- Do you want to know anything about the adoption process?
- Where should we go from here?
- Can we talk again? What is your phone number?
- Do you want to talk to my lawyer or a social worker about the adoption process? Should they call you? Do you want to call them?
  [John Doe (xxx) xxx-xxxx
  Sam Brown (xxx) xxx-xxxx]

Create your own list, keeping in mind a few basic premises. You will be very nervous; you may forget your name if it is not written down. The birth mother is just as nervous; you may have to fill the quiet. This is only an initial get-to-know-each-other call. The due date and what will happen next are the only issues that must be discussed. If the lead develops, there will be other chances to obtain additional details.

When the phone finally rings, the best advice is to be open, honest and sensitive. Let the birth mother control the conversation. If she needs to talk, listen; wants to listen, talk. Remind yourself that the two of you are very much alike—people going through the most difficult time in their lives.

Arranging to Fulfil Government Requirements

As mentioned in your provincial summary, there are various documents that must be submitted to the government during the adoption process. Many of these documents must be obtained by you or your adoption professionals. Documents such as medical examination reports, a financial statement, reference letters, a police check, a child abuse register search, and certificates of birth and marriage. Confirm with your adoption professional which documents you must obtain and when you must have them.

Some of the required documents are notifications to the relevant government authorities of various steps being taken or already taken by you as prospective adoptive parents. Often your adoption professional will file these notifications for you. Do not presume everything necessary has been done. If your adoption professional has not mentioned a particular notification set out in the provincial summary, ask him about it.

Depending on where you live and where your child is born, you may also have to complete an assessment and education process, often called a *homestudy*. Some provinces require a homestudy before a child is placed in your home; others allow the homestudy to be completed after the placement but before the adoption order is issued.

Ideally, the homestudy is a process that promotes increased self-understanding and personal growth. It is intended to educate applicants on parenting by adoption and determine their suitability to parent.

There are good arguments against the current homestudy process. No other prospective parents are asked to go through a similar process. Requiring compliance by only prospective adoptive parents suggests there is something suspect about wanting to parent an adopted child.

In addition, there is a serious conflict between the intended roles of the process—education and assessment. Since prospective adoptive parents want to appear completely comfortable with their adoption decision, they may not ask questions about the issues that concern them.

However, this is the system we must currently abide to adopt our children. Fighting for changes is best left for another day. One must simply get through the process. You may even be surprised and find it, as I did, more helpful and less intrusive than you thought it would be.

There is very little standardization with respect to homestudies. They are usually conducted by a social worker. The social worker may be an employee of the local public agency or a private practitioner. Generally, when a province allows prospective adoptive parents to hire a private practitioner, that social worker must meet specific educational or licensing requirements.

A homestudy can involve from one to several sessions over a period ranging from a day to several months. Generally, the sessions are private interviews, at least one of which is in your home. Sometimes, there are also group sessions.

Discussions are intended to draw out feelings about your present and past life and about your hopes for the future. General issues that may be addressed include your spouse's and your education, employment, family and medical history, personality traits, religion, interests and hobbies, finances, problem-solving and communication abilities, attitudes towards parenting and child rearing philosophies. Your marriage and the ability of you and your spouse to exist separately and as a team may also be assessed. Specific adoption concerns reviewed include the resolution of your infertility, your attitude towards adoption and your understanding of the differences in parenting by adoption.

How exhaustive a homestudy will be depends on the province and sometimes the region of the province or the social worker conducting the homestudy. Ask an adoptive parent in your community how they found the process. The imagined experience is probably far scarier than the reality.

If the homestudy is conducted after the child is in your home, the social worker will want to see how you and the child are adjusting to your new lives. If the homestudy is completed before placement, a separate post-placement review is generally scheduled for after the child arrives.

After the necessary sessions have been completed, the social worker prepares a report summarizing your discussions and his findings. Depending on when the homestudy is required, the report will conclude with a recommendation regarding the placement of a child in your home or the issuance of the adoption order.

Most social workers are not trying to catch you off guard. They are neither looking for skeletons nor judging your housekeeping skills. Some will want a complete tour of the house; some will only want to see the room where the child is or will be sleeping. Others will sit in a chair and not get up until it is time to leave.

You will probably be terrified during the first session. Consider yourself typical and try to stay as relaxed as possible. Offer her coffee. Think nothing of it, if she refuses. Do not be afraid to ask her any questions you have about the homestudy process or the adoption process in general.

Keep in mind that most homestudies go well. A negative recommendation is given only occasionally. If a child is already in a home, disruption will be a last resort. Even if the homestudy is being conducted before the placement, the process rarely reaches an actual negative end. Partway through the process, applicants usually realize that they are not ready, that there are concerns that must still be addressed. Therefore, as long as you are informed about the adoption world and stay true to your feelings, you should not be involved in the homestudy process until you are ready.

Ready, Set, Go

You are now ready to search for your child. You're not just ready; you're impatiently waiting to begin. You have spent a great deal of time learning about adoption. You just want to get going.

Hold on. There is just one more idea that must be stressed: you must sustain the excitement you are feeling. That excitement will provide you with the energy necessary to be constantly searching or thinking of new ways to search. It will allow you to be bold in asking for help. It will help you overcome your natural instinct to keep your inability to have children private.

How do you sustain that excitement? You must maintain what is behind the feeling—a strong desire to have a child and the belief that searching will soon cause that desire to be fulfilled. The desire to have a child will not easily fade or you would not have come this far. It is the belief in the potential for success that you must work hard at maintaining.

Hearing success stories should help. Let yourself be amazed at the unlikely ways in which adoptive parents have found their children. It is not like hearing that yet another friend or acquaintance is pregnant—emphasizing what you have not been able, and may never be able, to do. Each success story should give you new search ideas and new hope. The stories should emphasize that if you work hard, it will happen, and that it can happen any time.

Do not be too hard on yourself. Sustaining excitement does not mean that you have to be *up* every day. Some days will be harder than others. For days upon days, you will work hard and generate no leads. Keep going. Other days, you will generate lead after lead—all of which dissolve into nothing. Stay positive. Remember, you only need one successful lead and the harder you work, the greater the likelihood of finding that lead.

You will find many success stories in the pages that follow. If they are helpful, seek out more. Talk to adoptive parents you already know. Join an adoptive parent support group or subscribe to an adoption newsletter to meet others. Most adoptive parents remember what you are going through and are happy to help.

Start slowly. Read all of the search chapters. Note a few ideas that sound appealing to you. Go back to those sections and work through them in detail. Start a new approach when you are ready.

Many avenues are presented. There are many others. Do not let the seemingly endless amount of work overwhelm you. Instead, be encouraged that there is always something new to try.

Purchase a three-ring binder. Dutifully keep notes on everything you do and anything you might do.

Be creative. Work hard. Find your child.

chapter · · · · · · · · · · · · · · · · · 9

Networking

Networking is a complicated-sounding word with a simple meaning—exchanging information, contacts and experience within a group of people for professional or social purposes. In other words, people talk and listen, everyone benefits.

Everyone

Begin by simply talking and talking and . . . tell everyone that you are trying to adopt a child, that you are looking for a pregnant woman who is considering adoption for her unborn child. Tell every friend, acquaintance, business associate, shopkeeper, hairdresser. . . . Tell them to tell everyone they know.

Mary is quiet and very private. Yet she does not remember having any trouble telling people her and her husband, Bill, were trying to adopt a child. It was what she had to do and so she did it. She is sure that friends thought she was crazy when she told them she talked to her butcher and her dry-cleaner about their search. She talked to so many people that she and Bill have never been sure who was the initial contact in the adoption of their first, second or third child.

Everywhere you go, figure out a way to bring your search into the conversation. "Speaking of children . . . You'll never guess what's new . . . Have I told you what I'm trying to do? . . . Want to hear some good gossip? . . ."

Friends and acquaintances who are aware of your attempts to have a child, or who suspected there was a problem, will be thrilled. Your excitement will be contagious. They will be happy to help.

Strangers love to hear about things that are normally considered private. They also love to pass such information on to others. Privately adopting a child, and, specifically, actively searching for your child, is also relatively new. Other people will think it is fascinating. Giving them permission to gossip should not take away the fun of gossiping.

The first time you mention your search in a conversation, you will probably stumble over your words. You will be embarrassed. The second or third time will not be much better. By the time you've told a dozen people, you will be a pro.

Remember, believe in the possibility of success. Repeat to yourself, over and over, "I will find my child; I need only one successful lead." A few minutes of discomfort is nothing compared to the days, months and probably years of anguish caused by your inability to have a child.

Less than a month after Daphne and her husband, Ed, started seriously thinking about adoption, Daphne was sent on a training course by her employer. At the end of the course, during a goodbye dinner with a few new friends, Daphne gathered her courage and told everyone about their search. She mumbled something like, "I know you don't know anyone who is pregnant and is considering adoption and I'm sure you never will but . . . ah . . . I was told I should tell everyone and . . . well . . . just in case . . . ah . . . we could legally arrange . . . ah . . . call me." She left the dinner feeling silly and promptly forgot the conversation.

Six months later, Daphne and Ed received a card from someone who had heard about their search from one of Daphne's dinner companions. Three months later, their son was in their arms.

You will also be more comfortable with your search, if you remember that your success is also the success of a birth mother. You have found a child to love; she has found parents to love her child. She will probably thank you as much as you will thank her.

While waiting for a bus, Rebecca struck up a conversation with a young pregnant woman, Cindy, sitting beside her. When it came out that Cindy didn't know what to do about the baby, Rebecca mentioned her problems and the adoption search. Rebecca is now the adoptive mother of Cindy's birth child.

It is not necessary to ask the direct and uncomfortable question, "Do you know someone who is pregnant and considering adoption?" You simply tell people that you want to adopt a child—that you are looking for someone who is pregnant and considering adoption—and ask them to pass that information on to everyone they know and meet. Don't forget to also ask them if they can think of anyone else you should contact.

Depending on the circumstances, you may want to explain how private adoption works. Some people are misinformed. They have the impression that a private adoption is somehow shady or illegal. Mention in your explanation how it is advantageous, both for you and for a birth mother. Review Chapter 3 if you don't feel confident about your ability to inform.

Make sure that everyone you tell knows how to get in touch with you or your adoption professional. Ask them to pass on that contact information when they tell someone about your situation. Your birth mother letter is probably too detailed to leave with most casual contacts, but with each new contact consider whether leaving it may be helpful.

You may want to create a simplified version of your birth mother letter for such informal contacts. Another idea is to have business cards printed with, for example, you and your spouse's first names, an unlisted telephone number and the statements: "Adoption—a wonderful alternative. Call us collect anytime."

Make sure you review the search restrictions set out in the provincial summaries in Chapter 4. Look at whether you can network or advertise in your province and any other province where you want to search. If advertising is forbidden, ask your adoption professional how careful you should be about handing out birth mother letters or cards. There can be a fine line between networking and advertising; you do not want to cross it.

In addition to telling friends and acquaintances and everyone you happen to meet about your adoption, contact people you haven't seen in a few years. Look up friends from school or camp. Seek out old neighbours and lunch mates at former jobs. The further away your or their travels have taken them, the better.

Special Contacts

There are also specific people that you want to go out of your way to tell. You want to talk to anyone whose job or situation may bring them in contact with birth mothers.

Doctors

Often, the most helpful contacts are doctors, specifically, obstetricians, gynaecologists, and general practitioners. Many pregnant women contact a doctor when they are trying to decide what to do about their unborn child. Others do nothing until they arrive at the hospital ready to deliver. In both circumstances, the attending doctor has much influence.

Since doctors are often aware of several people looking to adopt a child, you must make yourself stand out. The most obvious way is to know the doctor or to meet the doctor in person, preferably after an introduction by a mutual acquaintance. Doctors are more likely to call someone they have met.

Andrea and Tony were at a dinner party with a few other couples. During a discussion about children, Andrea mentioned that they were just starting to consider adoption. They explained that if they did not want to wait years, they were going to have to actively search for their child.

The next day, a pregnant woman went to see her doctor. She told him that she wanted to place her child for adoption and asked if he could help. The doctor had also been at the dinner party. Although he had never met Andrea and Tony before the previous night, he obtained their telephone number from their mutual friend and called them. Andrea and Tony were successful before they had even started to search.

Meet with each of your own doctors. Give them a copy of your birth mother letter. Similarly, if you have any friends or relatives that are doctors, give them a copy of your letter. Remind them that you do not want privacy, that you want them to talk to their colleagues and, in fact, to anyone about your search.

Ask each doctor you know if they know of any other doctors you may contact. Also ask your friends and relatives if they know of any doctors you may contact. Personally contact as many as you can. Telephone the doctors, tell their secretaries who gave you their name and ask if they would call you when they have a minute. When your call is returned, explain why you are calling and ask if you could come in at the end or beginning of the day to say hello and drop off your birth mother letter.

Do not assume that doctors understand how private adoption works. Many do not. You may need to educate them. Even after your explanation, some will feel that they should not get involved. They may still be uncomfortable with private adoption. They may feel that they cannot suggest a particular person or couple as adoptive parents. Accept their hesitation and move on. Do not give up. Someone else will be glad to have options to discuss with their patients.

Many doctors will tell you that today very few babies are placed for adoption. Explain that you are aware of this fact but that you are still hopeful. Do not let them discourage you or distract you from completing your discussion with them.

Contact people, not institutions. You will probably get nowhere with a hospital or medical clinic administrator. Their main concern will be the policies and rules of the institution.

Remember to stay organized. Keep careful notes about the people you have contacted. List any information about the contact that may be useful later. For example, who is the mutual acquaintance, did you have a personal meeting, did you leave a birth mother letter.

* * *

While doctors are usually the best professional contacts, there are many others who may be of help in your search. Many of the issues raised with respect to the doctors will continue to be relevant. Three particularly important points are:

- Make sure the contacts remember you—if possible, meet with them, leave them your birth mother letter.
- Do not assume they understand how private adoption works—be prepared to educate them.
- Never leave without asking if they know of anyone else you may contact.

Adoption Professionals

The previously discussed adoption professionals, such as social workers or lawyers, may also be helpful in your search. However, they may not be as helpful as you think.

Adoption professionals usually have very long lists of people who want their help. They rarely are actively searching for birth mothers and, therefore, do not receive very many leads. Finally, many of their practices are *closed*—they only help the people who are using their full services. For example, if they get a lead, social workers will contact those people who have hired them to conduct counselling or a homestudy; lawyers will notify those people whose legal work they are going to complete.

Closing their practices makes sense when you remember that, generally, no one in Canada may be paid for simply making a match between birth and adoptive parents. However, there is no problem agreeing to use the adoption professional that leads you to your child to complete the adoption.

Do not misunderstand—there have been many situations where adoption professionals have helped. Do not, however, rely solely on them.

You may have compiled a list of adoption professionals in your community when you were investigating whom to hire. If not, glance at the discussion contained in Chapter 6. Call the adoption professionals and ask if they can help in your search. Explain that you are in the search phase of the process, that you do not need an information consultation or a homestudy. Be specific, ask them if they get unconnected birth mothers referred to them, unconnected in the sense that there are no prospective adoptive parents involved.

If the adoption professionals do talk to unconnected birth mothers, even if very few, and if they are willing to work with you, consider arranging to meet. They may suggest that sending a copy of your birth mother letter and, possibly, your homestudy is sufficient. However, given the number of prospective adoptive parents they talk to, they are more likely to remember you, if they have a face and a personality to match with your information. Keep in mind that they may want to be paid for the time they spend with you. Even if they cannot help, ask if they know of someone else who can.

Women's Clinics

Counsellors at women's clinics or centres that offer services such as pregnancy counselling and testing also have the potential to be helpful. Many pregnant women without a regular doctor or who do not want to face their own doctor search out such clinics.

The *Yellow Pages* telephone directory will name many of the clinics. Look under headings such as Birth Control Information, Pregnancy Counselling, and Women's Organizations & Services.

Be prepared to possibly encounter resistance. Historically, many pregnancy counsellors have not discussed adoption with their clients. Help them see that adoption is a desirable option for many clients and is an option that should be discussed with all clients.

Educational Institutions

High school, college or university teachers, guidance counsellors and nurses may also be of assistance in your search. Find staff who are sympathetic—staff whom the students look to for advice. As well, seek out staff who run special programs or courses for pregnant women.

Clergy

Similarly, ministers, priests, rabbis and other clergy are occasionally approached by women who want advice on unwanted pregnancies. A clergyman may be willing to raise adoption as an alternative, especially if you have a similar religious background.

Adoptive Parents

As previously discussed, adoptive parents understand what you are going through and are usually happy to help. Not only can they provide information and support but sometimes they can pass on a lead. Often, the networking and mailings of prospective adoptive parents continue to generate leads after they have found their child.

Contact friends and friends of friends who are adoptive parents. Ask to meet with them. Ask for names of other adoptive parents who may be able to help. Make new friends through your local adoption support group.

When Gina and Kevin told a friend that they were trying to adopt, they were introduced to Anne and Simon who had recently adopted. Anne and Simon met with Gina and Kevin and helped them get started.

Two months later, Anne heard about a pregnant woman who was considering adoption for her unborn child from a friend,

Laura, who had an adopted child and did not want any more children. At the time, Anne's daughter was only a few months old. Since the laws of her province did not allow her to adopt another child that soon, she called Gina and Kevin.

You should now have a long list of people who may be able to help in the search for your child. Diligently work down the list: recording those you have contacted, adding more and more names. At the same time, keep talking to everyone you meet—talk and talk and . . .

chapter · · · · · · · · · · · · · · · · 10

Mailings

Ideally, you should meet each person who can possibly help in the search for your child. Realistically, this is impossible. Many potential contacts will not live in your city, perhaps, not even in your province. As well, if you have diligently followed Chapter 9 and talked and talked—you will have a long list of potential contacts. Time constraints may prevent you from meeting them all.

Do not ignore the contacts you cannot meet personally. Whenever possible, use the mail to tell them of your search.

There are two types of mailings. You can write to people you know or whose names you have been given by common acquaintances. Or you can write what is sometimes called a *cold* letter to unknown persons whose name you have obtained by virtue of their profession.

Review the provincial summaries found in Chapter 4. Check if your province, and any province where you wish to search, allows the use of one or both types of mailings.

If you are permitted to do both types of mailing, first concentrate on writing known or referred contacts. Doctors, adoption professionals and other people whose jobs or situation bring them in contact with birth mothers generally receive many letters from prospective adoptive parents. Knowing the letter recipient or having a mutual acquaintance is akin to a personal meeting. It allows you to stand out from everyone else who is asking for help in the search for their child. It should cause your request to go to the top of the pile.

This does not mean that writing cold letters is a waste of time, just that you should be realistic when deciding how your time should be allocated. Obviously, the more people you contact, the greater your chances of finding a lead.

Creating a Cover Letter

Generally, your mailing should consist of your birth mother letter and a cover letter. Your cover letter will introduce you and your search. It will explain how you hope the birth mother letter will be used.

You have spent a lot of time creating your birth mother letter. Do not ignore the cover letter. It is also important. If it is poorly written, it and the enclosed birth mother letter will probably be ignored or discarded; your effort will have been wasted.

Figures 3 and 4 show two sample cover letters. The letters were used by two couples who are now adoptive parents.

As with each of the sample letters, your cover letter should contain four basic ideas. First, explain why you are writing the letter. You want to adopt a child. You cannot give birth to a child. You need help in your search.

Second, outline the type of help you need. You want your birth mother letter, but not the cover letter with your identifying information, given to any pregnant woman considering adoption. You want your search discussed with colleagues and anyone else who can possibly help.

Third, reassure that you are prepared to adopt legally and quickly without sacrificing the needs of the birth mother or the recipient of the letter. You are working with adoption professionals and, if possible, have arranged for birth mother counselling. You have completed the required preparations. You will keep any help confidential.

Finally, state how you can be contacted. Provide for direct contact with yourself and, depending on the arrangement with your adoption professionals, indirect contact through a professional.

Newsletters

Your cover letter and birth mother letter is sometimes too formal an introduction to your search. There may be circumstances where a chatty one-page newsletter would be better. For example, old camp or school mates who live in different cities would love to get a newsletter talking about what's going on in your life, your adoption search and any other available gossip. Include the information contained in the cover letter in a less formal manner. Also attach a copy of your birth mother letter and ask them to give it to anyone that could possibly help.

Figure 3

Tom and Mary Jones
123 Anystreet
Anytown, Anyplace

January 15, xxxx

Mr. Lawyer
456 Anystreet
Anytown, Anyplace

Dear Mr. Lawyer,

Janet Smith suggested that my husband, Tom, and I write to you. We are good friends of Janet and she thought you may be able to help in our search to adopt a child.

We cannot have a natural child. Although we are aware that very few babies are placed for adoption, we hope to be the lucky parents of one of them.

If you should become aware of a pregnant woman who is considering adoption for her unborn child, we would be very grateful if you would give her the enclosed letter and, if she wishes to see what we look like, the enclosed photograph. Since we wish to remain anonymous at this time, we would appreciate it if you would keep this covering letter confidential.

We are working with a licensed social worker who is available to make all the necessary arrangements for adoption and would ensure that the birth mother receives counselling. Since our home study is nearly complete, we can act on very short notice.

Thank you for taking the time to read this letter. Please feel free to discuss its contents with your colleagues or anyone else who may be able to help. In addition, if you have any suggestions on who else we may contact, please let us know.

Should you wish to contact us, please call us at our home anytime at (xxx) xxx-xxxx or call our social worker, Jim Jacket, at (xxx) xxx-xxxx.

Yours sincerely,
Mary Jones

Figure 4

---

789 Anystreet
Anytown, Anyplace
Home: xxx-xxx-xxxx
Office: xxx-xxx-xxxx

January 15, xxxx

Dr. Green
124 Anystreet
Anytown, Anyplace

Dear Dr. Green,

We are writing to ask for your help in our search to adopt a baby.

My husband and I have always wanted a family and when we discovered that we had fertility problems we decided that we would do everything possible to adopt a baby. The enclosed letter to a prospective birth mother provides information about both of us.

We want to assure you of complete confidentiality in the event that you are able to assist us. Our Adoption Home Study has been completed and our social worker will look after both pre and post natal counselling as well as the legal process involved in completing an adoption.

If an appropriate situation arises in your practice, or in that of one of your colleagues, please detach this letter and give the enclosed letter to the prospective birth mother. Perhaps it will help a woman decide what to do if she is unsure of her options.

We can be reached at either of the above telephone numbers. If you are calling long distance please call collect and if no one is available please leave a message and we will return your call. Or, if you prefer, you can call our social worker, Mike Tucker, at (xxx) xxx-xxxx.

Sincerely,
Sharon Jones
Alan Smith

Sending Cold Letters

Once you have exhausted your supply of referred contacts, you may want to write cold letters to the adoption professionals, doctors or other professionals whose names you have obtained. Remember to confirm that your province, and any province where you wish to search, does not forbid such mailings. If you decide to proceed, consider the following additional issues.

Each letter should still be addressed to a specific recipient. Since word processing packages allow the name of a letter recipient to be easily changed, the less personal *Dear Sir / Madam* letter should be avoided whenever possible.

Since by definition a cold letter does not contain an introduction, you should try to make yourself stand out in another way. One couple decided that an honest plea was best:

> We are very sure that you receive many such requests and we know that there are many couples like ourselves who desperately want a child. To be honest, many people cautioned us that we are simply wasting our time in sending out letters to doctors like yourself. But at ages 34 and 35, we are rapidly running out of time, and we need to appeal to everyone who can help. . . . I am sure you can appreciate how much anguish and effort has gone into our search for a child to make our lives complete. Without the help of people like you, we may never know the joys of parenting. Please think of us.

One doctor who received this letter, did just that. He called the couple when one of his patients was considering adoption for her unborn child.

If you want names of professionals to whom cold letters may be sent, go to your local library. Names and addresses of various professionals in your province (doctors, lawyers) can be obtained from yearly professional publications. The library may also have the *Yellow Pages* telephone directory of other cities.

One adoptive parent created a computer diskette containing the names and addresses of all obstetricians, gynaecologists and general practitioners in Ontario. Other similar diskettes may exist. Ask all of your new friends in the adoptive parents network you have started to create. An adoptive parent who has such a diskette should be happy to make you a copy.

*   *   *

One final thought with respect to mailings. Be aware that the recipient of your letter may forget your request and give both your cover letter and birth mother letter to a birth mother. The birth mother will then know your full name and address, whether or not you intended her to know.

There is not much you can do to prevent such carelessness. Do not staple or otherwise attach your cover and birth mother letters. Make sure your request that only the birth mother letter be given to a birth mother is clearly stated in the cover letter.

If you have decided that you want a confidential adoption, and still feel the same way once there is a live birth mother in the picture, you can always decide not to proceed further with that particular birth mother.

*　*　*

Your search for your child is well underway. You should feel good. You are actively trying to create your family. You are not simply sitting and waiting for something to happen. You are working hard to make it happen. Keep working. It *will* happen.

chapter · · · · · · · · · · · · · · · **11**

Advertising

The idea of using advertising to find a birth mother causes some people discomfort; probably because advertising is generally considered a commercial tool. However, it is simply a tool—a tool that helps people find each other.

Personals have been around for years and have become a popular method of finding a date, a friend, a spouse. Why not a child?

Before you begin, review the provincial summaries found in Chapter 4. Make sure your province, and any province where you wish to search, allows the use of advertising in an adoption.

Placing Your Ad

There are many places to advertise. You are probably most familiar with the daily city newspapers. There are also more than 500 weekly community newspapers in Canada.

Advertising in community newspapers is an effective way of reaching pregnant women who live outside the urban centres. Such women may not have access to women's clinics and may, therefore, not be aware of their options.

In certain provinces, with one phone call or fax, you can place an ad that will be run simultaneously in many community newspapers in the province. Check on the availability of blanket classified advertising with your local community newspaper or with your province's Community Newspapers Association.

Lisa wrote an ad expressing her desire to adopt a child. She arranged for the ad to be run once in all of the weekly community newspapers in her province. She had four responses; none developed further than a few telephone calls. She decided to rerun the ad two weeks later. Again, she had four responses. This time, one of those responses led her to her son.

University and college newspapers may be a good place for your ad. The Canadian Federation of Students publishes a Student Association Directory each year that includes the contact information for every school's newspaper.

Think. Where else can you advertise? Does your profession have a newspaper? Do you, or does someone you know, work for a company that has its own internal newspaper? Do you speak a second language—is there a newspaper published in that language in your province?

Your ad does not have to be read by a birth mother to be effective. You may, for example, want to place it in a newspaper or magazine specifically written for doctors, nurses, social workers, lawyers or any other professionals who come into contact with birth mothers. Check with the relevant professional organization, if you do not know the name of their newspaper or magazine.

Newspapers and magazines are not the only way to advertise. You can place an ad on a bulletin board. Many churches, community centres, supermarkets and even laundromats have bulletin boards. You can print up flyers and have them distributed.

Do not be shy. Advertising really does work—sometimes in the most unusual of circumstances.

Tom called a local community newspaper about placing his adoption search ad in the newspaper. He was asked if he would like to run it in an additional nine commonly owned newspapers for a small additional cost. Tom agreed without even asking the names of the other newspapers. The birth mother of Tom's son answered one of his ads. She saw it in a local Buy and Sell *newspaper right under an ad selling a used computer.*

Adoption ads are now quite common. A newspaper may still, however, refuse to run it. Other newspapers may require a letter from your adoption professional stating that you are involved in a legal adoption.

In deciding to place an ad in a particular publication, you may want to consider whether it will be the only adoption ad in that edition. Even if your ad is fabulous, after she has read ten others, a birth mother may think yours sounds just like all the others. Some newspapers will guarantee exclusivity for the day your ad is run.

On the other hand, one adoptive parent felt that a newspaper with many adoption ads was like a shopping mall with many shops. Since she would rather shop at a mall where she had a lot of choices, she thought a pregnant woman looking for a home for her unborn child might similarly want to look in a place where she had a lot of choices.

Once you have decided to place an ad in a particular publication, request that a copy of the issue containing your ad be sent to you. This allows you to check for any errors in the ad and have a memento from the beginning of the successful search for your child.

Writing Your Ad

Before you write your ad, read as many as you can. You will discover that although many ads sound similar, you like certain phrases and dislike others.

Figure 5 on page 148 contains some examples. Look for others. One easily available source is *US Magazine*. Go to your public library and ask to look at several back issues. Look under *Adoption* in the Classified listings found at the back of the magazine.

Some adoptive parents think the ad should be short and simple, others think it will stand out if it is long and flowery. As with everything else, there is no right answer. Write what sounds good to you.

Dealing with Problem Calls

Although crank calls are possible, they do not appear to be a major problem. If you do receive one, there are a few actions you may take.

One telephone company, after consultation with the police, suggests that you react to a crank call by (i) hanging up without speaking and (ii) removing the phone from its cradle for a time. Crank callers generally give up when they receive no reaction. In addition, some telephone companies have new technology that allows you to initiate a trace from your telephone. The address of the caller is then supplied to the police. Talk with your telephone company, if you have concerns.

It is more likely that you will receive calls from pregnant women who want advice on what they should do. Obviously, you are in an awkward situation. You want to encourage them to obtain help so that they can decide what is best for them. You also want them to consider you as the adoptive parent, if they decide that adoption is the right choice for them. You must simply try to strike the right balance.

Figure 5

Adoption? Pregnant? Young, fun-loving couple wishes to adopt newborn baby. Strictly legal and confidential. Call Jody and Tim collect (xxx) xxx-xxxx.

A LOVING CHOICE: Do you imagine warm hugs, story time & family fun? Perhaps we share the same vision for your baby's life. Call Tom/Jane xxx-xxx-xxxx.

Are you bright, courageous, love life? Me too! Not ready to be a Mom? I am! Financially secure, educated, professional single woman who loves books/music/outdoors and eager to share her every joy with a child. Expenses paid as legal. Call Jane xxx-xxx-xxxx or lawyer May Sims xxx-xxx-xxxx.

College-educated, financially secure couple unable to have baby wishes to adopt. Let us help you through this difficult time. Call collect (xxx) xxx-xxxx.

Pregnant? A warm loving couple is anxious to adopt and provide a home for your unborn child. Working with government licensed agency. Confidentiality assured. Call collect (xxx) xxx-xxxx.

Part III

Putting It All Together

chapter....................**12**

Your Search Is Over—
Now What?

You have found her—the woman that you hope will be the birth mother of your child. She may be early in her pregnancy, due any day or anywhere in between. You are so excited that you cannot think about anything else. Yet you don't want to deal with it, for fear that you will make a mistake. What are you supposed to do? How are you supposed to cope?

Dealing with the Emotional Turmoil

The search for the birth mother of your child was likely a frustrating road to travel. Yet, waiting for the birth will probably provide a bumpier ride. Searching kept you busy; it made the time pass quickly. Unless the birth mother's due date is imminent, the wait will provide too much time for thinking and worrying. You must recognize this fact and deal with it in the best way that you can.

You are going to jump back and forth between feelings of ecstasy and terror. So much depends on the birth mother. How can you not analyze every word she says and every action she takes. One minute you will think everything is terrific; the next minute you will think she is wavering in her decision.

Or maybe no decision has been made. You are in the midst of talking to a pregnant woman considering adoption and everything seems to be going fine. Yet she wants time to think. What are you to do? Exactly what she wants you to do; give her time.

I am a fatalist; so are most of the adoptive parents I know. Do

not misunderstand me. I do not think that everything is so predeter-
mined that you may as well sit back and do nothing. I believe you
must do the best you can; then if it was meant to happen, it will
happen.

Before my husband and I began our adoption search, I probably
would have laughed at such an idea. The theory developed as a self-
preservation tool to keep me sane. I needed to believe that my child
was out there waiting for me; so I did. It took me off the hook, let
me work as hard as I could and then leave the rest to destiny. If a
lead did not work out for any reason, that child was not meant to
be my child. My child was still waiting for me.

Now that I have my son, I am convinced that the theory is right.
I cannot imagine anyone else being my son; no one else could be my
son. Everything I went through was necessary to get me to my son.

If you have not yet read my previously mentioned essay about the
emotional side of my adoption experience, *Tears for My Son*, this
might be a good time to do so. It can be found at the end of the book.
Maybe it will help you believe that your child is waiting for you.

I am not trying to tell you that if the birth mother chooses others
to be the adoptive parents of her child or decides to parent herself,
you will not be devastated; you will. I am simply saying that you
will be able to go on; you will be able to try again—perhaps not tomor-
row or next week, but soon.

These are not just words. I know of what I write. As I wrote in
Tears for My Son, a few months before our son was born, a child we
thought *would be* our son was born. Two days after the birth, the
birth mother changed her mind and decided to parent.

There are a few practical things you can do to help ease the stress.
First, do not be considerate of your family and friends. Do exactly
what is right for you. If you don't want to go to yet another baby
shower, don't go. If you don't want to hear about little Jimmy's wonderful doings, change the topic. Remember these people care about
you; they will understand.

Also, consider lying about your adoption progress. My husband
and I told everyone about that first major lead. It was our way of
being pregnant and sharing the good news. When the birth mother
changed her mind, the pain seemed to last forever, since we then
had to share the bad news.

When the second lead came along, we told no one but our parents.
Even they were given strict instructions not to ask us for the latest
news on the lead, that updates would be provided as matters developed. Anyone else who asked us about our search was told "nothing
is happening yet."

Once our son was literally in our arms, we called our siblings and closest friends. Everyone understood. Your friends and family will understand. Do what is best for you.

Similarly, hesitate before doing those prospective parent tasks: choosing a name, reading infant care books, buying baby clothes and furniture or decorating a nursery. Consider whether you want to do the task given the fact that you may not have found your child yet. Figure out what gives you pure joy and what will be too much to handle, if things go wrong.

Some prospective adoptive parents find using a name to refer to their unborn child a painless way to make the experience seem real. Others find it makes that child too real—leading to extra pain and the need to find another name, if the adoption plan falls apart.

Reading about a child's first few weeks allows prospective parents to mentally prepare for the arrival of their child—a good idea for all prospective parents. However, it also increases anticipation and excitement—not a good idea for all prospective parents. You must decide that the experience is worth any extra suffering, if the arrival does not happen when expected.

Similarly, will a room full of baby paraphernalia drive you crazy or give you hope? Do not think that since you need certain items, you have no choice. You could purchase the necessities and leave them in a friend's basement or pick out items at stores that will deliver with a few days' notice. Or you could arrange to borrow the necessities for the first few weeks.

When my husband and I received the phone call telling us that the first birth mother had changed her mind, we were painting animals on the wall of the nursery. We did not put away our paint and lock the door, as I would have predicted, but worked long into the night to finish. I know our friends were uncomfortable when we proudly showed off the nursery waiting for our child, whoever he or she might be. Yet it made us feel good.

You must find the balance that works for you. Do only what feels right. Catch up on everything else later.

All this talk about things going wrong. It could happen; it might happen. I guarantee you, though, the reward is worth the risk. Be sensible. Try, as much as you can, to protect yourself from being hurt. However, do not be so paranoid that you cannot function or you function with little joy or hope.

Working with the Birth Mother

There are several items that should, whenever possible be discussed with the birth mother, prior to the birth. There is no set schedule to follow. You must gauge the stage of the relationship and proceed accordingly.

You or your adoption professionals will want to explore with the birth mother her health and social history and the involvement of the birth father. It is often easier if the adoption professionals discuss these issues. They will have less difficulty asking the tough questions. The previously discussed counselling and independent legal advice as well as medical treatment during the pregnancy should also be addressed.

You may want to start her thinking about the birth. Does she have a hospital picked out? Who will be her coaches? Does she want you in the labour room, waiting outside or not be present at all?

Similarly, she must consider what is to happen after the birth. Does she want to spend time with the child or leave the hospital without seeing the child? Who will call you when she goes into labour or the child is born? May you visit her and the child in the hospital or need you wait until she leaves? Who is to take care of the child in the hospital? Where will the child go after being discharged from the hospital?

Encourage her to use a counsellor to sort out what she wants. Obviously, she may change her mind about any particular detail. Yet, you will be able to create an initial birth plan.

Try not to interpret any decisions as an indicator of disaster. For example, some birth mothers need time to say goodbye to their child. Wanting to spend time with her child in the hospital does not translate into having doubts about the adoption plan.

Having the birth mother review, with a counsellor, what is to happen at the time of the birth has additional advantages. The walk through will help make the adoption real; it will cause the birth mother to feel some of the love and grief that will surface at the time of the birth. Feeling these emotions before the birth may help lessen the load at the time of birth. It will also allow the counsellor to make sure the birth mother understands that she should be feeling such emotions, that those feelings need not mean she is making the wrong decision.

You, your spouse and the birth mother must also discuss your relationship, what it will be both before and after the birth. Generally, you should try hard to comply with anything the birth mother wants before the birth. It is a short period of time, almost anything you can do to make it easier for her is warranted. If she wants to talk with you regularly, talk. If she wants a meeting, meet. If she wants you to leave her alone, step back.

Obviously, every birth mother is different. What she will want cannot be predicted. However, you should realize that more and more birth mothers are asking to meet the prospective adoptive parents of their child.

If the thought of a meeting causes you concern, imagine how she must feel. She has the same fears as you: Will you like each other? Will you want to continue with the adoption plan? But she is also worried that you will judge her, that because of her predicament you will find her wanting.

Try to look at her desire for a meeting in a cold rational light. First, a meeting will provide you with impressions to share with your child—impressions that may someday be cherished. In addition, keep in mind that you want something from the birth mother: you want to adopt her child. There are many other prospective adoptive parents for that child. You need her to like you, to choose you, to feel confident about the adoption plan. It is to your advantage to make yourself real to her, to go through the awkwardness of a meeting so that she feels comfortable with you.

Why should she suffer through the discomfort of a meeting? She could simply hand over the child to a social worker and disappear. The social worker could confidently assure her that the child would receive loving adoptive parents. Yet she wants to meet you. Why? There is only one plausible answer. She cares about her unborn child.

She wants to know that you and your spouse will be good parents. She needs to know that she is making the right decision. Being told is not good enough; she wants to see for herself.

No one would hire a baby sitter without meeting and knowing something about that person. How can someone be expected to not only leave her child with a stranger, but to give that child to a stranger?

Instead of being upset that the possible birth mother of your child wants to meet you, be impressed. Adoption is not an easy choice, even without a meeting. With abortion, a pregnancy can be hidden from a sometimes cruel world. With parenting, no one is considered to have "given away their own flesh and blood." Those that choose adoption for their children must be mature enough to deal with such pressures. They must be dedicated to doing what is right for their children and themselves.

Now add the fact that she wants to subject herself to the extra discomfort of a meeting to ensure that adoption by you is the right decision for her child. Don't discourage her; commend her.

A meeting may involve only you, your spouse and the birth mother or there may be additional people to consider. In our first experience, a friend of the birth mother arranged and attended the meeting. At the meeting with the birth mother of our son, the birth mother's parents were present. Obviously, there may be a birth father involved.

In addition, it is possible to have an adoption professional present at the meeting.

The presence of an adoption professional could increase the comfort level of the parties by, for example, prompting conversation during any lapses. However, knowing that a professional is listening to the conversation could also increase any discomfort. Discuss with your adoption professionals and the birth mother what is best for all of you. A middle ground is possible by, for example, having a professional spend the first few minutes in the room and then leave.

At the meeting, keep in mind the advice given in Chapter 8 with respect to your first conversation with a birth mother: be open, honest and sensitive. Accept that it will be awkward and try minimizing the discomfort by remembering the following facts. The birth mother is just like you—an ordinary person going through the most difficult time in her life. She is also feeling nervous and awkward. Other than following normal rules of courtesy and respect, there are no right or wrong things to say or ways to act. You would not have got this far if she did not like what she already knows about you.

Besides addressing what the birth mother wants before the birth, you must begin to discuss the type of relationship she wants after the birth. You need to make sure that you and your spouse can live with whatever she wants or that she can accept your limitations. Does she want to exchange letters or meet regularly? Does she want a full disclosure of identifying information?

As previously mentioned, the type of involvement being discussed is generally called *openness*. The lines of communication between the birth parents, the adoptive parents and the adoptee are being opened.

You may have heard the term *open adoption*. This term is used inconsistently. Some suggest that an adoption can only be considered an open adoption when the birth and adoptive families have (i) met each other, (ii) exchanged identifying information, and (iii) as much ongoing contact, whether in person or through letters, as they want. When there is a lesser degree of openness, they consider the adoption *semi-open*. To others, an open adoption is an adoption with any degree of openness. Make sure you know exactly what degree of openness is being discussed by the birth mother.

It is interesting to note that most adoptive parents seem to be comfortable with exactly the amount of openness that exists in their adoption. Any more seems frightening, any less a loss. Yet, many of those adoptive parents were initially reluctant to have any openness in their adoption.

If you still feel uncomfortable with the idea of some type of relationship with the birth mother, do some additional research. Reread the discussion found in Chapter 2. Use Lois Melina and Sharon Roszia's terrific book, *The Open Adoption Experience*,[1] to guide you through the steps that would occur. Glance at one of the books listed in Appendix III that explain the theories behind openness in adoption. Finally, talk to adoptive parents; allow yourself to be comforted by their successful relationships with the birth parents of their children.

One final issue that you may want to broach with the birth mother is naming the child. At the time of the birth, the birth mother is the legal parent of the child. She fills out a government form registering the fact of the birth and the names given to the child. There is nothing to stop you from changing the child's first and middle names along with the family name when the adoption order is issued some months later. However, depending on the relationship you have with the birth mother, you may want to include her in the naming decision.

Some birth mothers are simply curious about the names you have chosen; others request a say. The birth mother of your child may, for instance, want you to keep a name chosen by her as a middle name.

Allowing her to choose a name or including her in your decision has an advantage. The birth mother may use the chosen names when filling out the initial government forms. There is then no need to change your child's names; he begins life with his chosen names.

Completing the Necessary Details

As the time of birth approaches, you should consider finding a paediatrician. You will want your doctor to examine the child as soon as possible and since some paediatricians will visit the child in the hospital, it makes sense to find one you like before the birth.

Re-read the government requirements addressed in chapters 4 and 8. Make sure everything that needs to be done before the placement of the child in your home has been completed or is in the process of being finished.

Finally, confirm that you and your adoption professionals have made all of the necessary arrangements for the birth and the days that follow. While reading the next chapter, jot down any preparations that still need to be made or details that have not yet been confirmed. Try to ensure that the only remaining surprise is whether you have a son or daughter.

Endnote

[1] Melina, Lois Ruskai and Sharon Kaplan Roszia. *The Open Adoption Experience*. New York: Harper, 1993.

Your Child Is Born

Finally, the moment that you sometimes thought would never happen: the birth of your child, the start of a new chapter in your life. The emptiness you have felt can finally start to be filled up with bottles and diapers and spit-up and . . .

It Ain't Over 'Til It's Over

Unlike most parents, you could be doing almost anything when your child is born. However, whether you are in the labour room, pacing in the hallway, waiting by the telephone or just going about your daily life, hearing about the birth is pure magic. Life is suddenly wonderful. Tears of joy wash away any remnants of pain endured. Your heart pounds with excitement and anticipation.

After a few minutes or, if you are lucky, several hours, terror may start to dull your exhilaration. As previously discussed, immediately after the birth is the hardest period for the birth mother and, hence, for you. She has abruptly shifted from being pregnant to being a mother. Everything is suddenly real to her—the child and the decision not to parent that child.

Generally, this is the heart of the adoption plan. If the birth mother can stay firm in her resolve during the first few days after the birth, the adoption plan will probably succeed.

Although it is almost impossible during this time to think about anything but the adoption, try. Keep as busy as you can. What a great time to clean out your closets, rearrange your furniture or freeze some home-cooked meals.

Unfortunately, you will likely not feel completely free of fear until the adoption order is issued. However, as you proceed down the road, the terror will subside. Being a parent will keep you too busy and too happy to think about anything but success. Yet a little weight will lift off your shoulders as each milestone is met—bringing the child home, the signing of the consent and, in certain provinces, the expiry of the consent withdrawal period. Then suddenly it will be over; your child will legally be your child.

At the Hospital

Depending on your relationship with the birth mother, you may be at the hospital during or immediately after the birth. Every hospital has different policies with respect to adoptions. Some are terrific: They allow the prospective adoptive parents to spend as much time with the child as they and the birth mother want; they leave the choice as to whether the child stays in the nursery or the birth mother's room up to the birth mother. Other hospitals have set procedures that the staff refuse to bend or break.

Well before the birth mother's due date, make sure you know what can or must happen in the hospital (i) at the birth, (ii) during the birth mother's and the child's stay, and (iii) when the birth mother and the child are ready to leave. You do not want to discover at the last minute that plans carefully made by you and the birth mother cannot be put into place. Nor do you want to find out at midnight on a Saturday that an official letter is required to let you in to see your newborn. Doing your homework allows you to concentrate on the important aspects of the birth experience: the child, the birth mother and you.

It is important not to forget the birth mother. Both the birth and the reality of the impending separation from her birth child are traumatic experiences. She needs to see that you care about her as well as the child.

Discuss with your adoption professionals whether you may bring the birth mother a small gift. If you are told that anything you give may be considered an illegal payment, give nothing and explain the rules to the birth mother. It was stressed to me and my husband that even sending flowers could be interpreted as attempting to influence her decision. Rather than be embarrassed at arriving empty-handed at the hospital, we relayed our dilemma before the birth. She understood; we even shared a snicker at the stupidity of such rigidness.

Expect the birth mother to want changes to the agreed upon plans. The plans were based on how she thought she would feel after the birth; she likely feels a little different. However, that does not necessarily mean that she no longer wants to go through with the adoption.

Remember, it is common and even healthy for the birth mother to spend time with the child. She needs to tell him she loves him, to explain that the adoption is the right plan for everyone, to say goodbye.

It is impossible not to worry. However, try to remain as calm and as understanding as possible. Whatever changes are requested, the birth mother is not trying to make it harder on you. She is simply concerned about herself and her decisions.

Similarly, be easy on yourself. Don't worry if you do not feel an immediate bond with the child. Some parents, by birth or adoption, feel that bond immediately; some require time for the child to find its way into their hearts.

If the plan includes you caring for the child, do not expect yourself to be competent. Parenting a newborn is not an innate ability but rather a skill that you will quickly learn. The first time I changed my son's diaper, it took me almost fifteen minutes. He was screaming at being exposed for so long and the more he screamed the more I seemed to fumble. By the time we left the hospital, I was an expert.

Ask to receive any instructional information the hospital provides to new parents. There are often pamphlets and videos that provide step-by-step directions on various topics—from feeding to bathing. Sometimes, there are even classes in the nursery.

Bringing Your Child Home

Before the birth, discuss with your adoption professional, what is to happen after the child leaves the hospital. Even if you and the birth mother want the baby to go directly home with you, this is not always possible.

Remember, the birth mother, and sometimes the birth father, must sign a consent to the adoption. Each province specifies how soon after the birth that consent may be signed. Some provinces allow the child to go directly into the home of the prospective adoptive parents, no matter when the consent is to be signed. Other provinces do not allow the placement until after the consent is signed. If the signing cannot take place until several days after the birth and the child cannot stay in the hospital during that time, the child may need to have a temporary home. Often the child may stay with a family acceptable to both the prospective adoptive parents and the birth parents. The summaries set out in Chapter 4 list the provincial stipulations.

As well, there are circumstances when an adoption professional will suggest that a child spend a short time in a foster home. Perhaps the birth mother has been wavering in her decision to proceed with the adoption or maybe she wants to see the child a few times before signing the consent. A temporary placement may be best for all. It could, for example, allow both the prospective adoptive parents and the birth mother to spend time with the child until either the consent to adoption is signed or the time to withdraw the consent has elapsed.

If you are going to pick up your child and bring her home, there are few things you should remember to take with you. A car seat is a necessity if you are coming home by car, helpful if arriving by airplane or train. You will also need bottles filled with formula, diapers, receiving blankets for wrapping the baby, a camera with extra film and batteries and several newborn sleepers. If the trip is to last several days, keep in mind that you also need clothes and toiletries.

Celebrating. When should you tell your friends and family you have a child? When should you announce it to the world? As with so many decisions, there is no right answer. Do what feels best for you. As previously discussed, I condone lying about the possibility of your child until the last minute. However, once that child is in your home, keeping a low profile will probably not protect you from any pain. Share your joy. Celebrate your new love with your close friends and family.

If the consent to adoption withdrawal period applying to your adoption is a set number of days, you may want to wait until the expiry of the period before telling the rest of the world. The relief from passing this milestone may be worth a slight delay in placing the announcement in the newspaper or having a party or religious ceremony.

Completing the Adoption

You have entered the home stretch. The child is in your home, the consent to adoption has been signed and, where applicable, the period for withdrawing the consent has passed. You are in what is sometimes called the *probationary period*—a set number of months before the adoption order may be issued.

Your major concern in the next few months must and should be your child. However, do not ignore the final steps required to legally complete the adoption.

Stay on top of the government requirements discussed in Chapters 4 and 8. Make sure that your adoption professional is filing any necessary notifications and applications as soon as permitted by law. This will ensure issuance of the adoption order as soon as possible.

That order is important. In some provinces, it signifies the end of the consent withdrawal period. In all provinces, it is the basis for your legal claim to your child.

The adoption order is issued after a hearing by a judge. Generally, the hearing is an informal affirmation of a decision made by the government department responsible for adoptions—a decision that you are aware of long before the hearing. You may have the choice whether to attend. My husband and I chose not to attend. Braeden was already our son; he had been our son for almost a year. The issuance of the order was simply a formality that proved this fact to the rest of the world.

chapter • • • • • • • • • • • • • • • • **14**

Looking Past the Adoption

Once you have become a parent, even if not yet a legal parent, you must begin to look past the adoption. You must address the issues that are faced by all new parents and those that are unique to families created by adoption.

Taking a Leave from Work

You and your spouse should consider whether one or both of you will take a leave from work when your child comes home. When discussing your options, keep in mind two separate issues: job security and unemployment insurance benefits.

In Canada, all employees and employers are governed by legislation respecting employment standards. These standards provide the necessary job security when an employee wants a leave from work. The standards stipulate the minimum amount of unpaid leave an employer must allow an employee in various circumstances, such as maternity or adoption. Generally, the standards state that the employee is entitled to reinstatement in the same position, or in a comparable one, at not less than the wages and benefits accrued before the leave.

Most employees and employers are governed by their provincial employment standards legislation. For instance, an employee working in British Columbia is entitled to the benefits provided under the B.C. Employment Standards Act. However, when an employer's business crosses provincial boundaries—financial institutions, telecommunication and transportation companies—a federal act, the Canada Labour Code, governs.

All of the jurisdictions stipulate a mother by birth is entitled to an unpaid maternity leave of seventeen or eighteen weeks. These provisions do not apply to adoptive mothers. A few jurisdictions do have specific provisions for adoptive parents. However, most jurisdictions deal with adoptive parents by allowing every parent, birth or adoptive, mother or father, to have an unpaid parental leave of a set number of weeks. Generally, maternity and parental leaves are not mutually exclusive; a mother by birth may take a parental leave immediately following her maternity leave. The only jurisdiction that does not provide job security to adoptive parents is the Yukon Territory.

Generally, there are notification and length-of-service requirements. There may be other conditions such as a maximum age for an adopted child or a date by which the leave must have commenced.

Keep in mind that the only issue being discussed is job security—how much time you can take off and still come back to the same or a similar job. Also remember that these are minimum standards. Some employers by inclination or negotiation allow more time off; they cannot, however, allow less.

Review the chart found on the next page and talk to your employer. If you have any concerns use the government listings—the *blue* pages—of your telephone book to contact your local Employment or Labour Standards Office. If you think you are governed by the federal legislation, call your local Canada Labour Office instead.

The second issue you must consider is being paid for the leave. An employer may pay all or a portion of an employee's wages during a permitted leave as part of a benefits package. Otherwise, an employer is not required by law to make such payments.

An employee is, however, entitled to public assistance—unemployment insurance benefits—during maternity and parental leaves from work. These benefits are covered under federal legislation. Therefore all Canadians, no matter which province they live in, are entitled to the same benefits during their leave. The benefits cover 60 percent of wages up to a maximum amount for a certain number of weeks.

A mother by birth is entitled to fifteen weeks of maternity benefits. The mother and father of a child, by birth or by adoption, are entitled to ten weeks of parental benefits between them. Again, these benefits are not mutually exclusive; a mother by birth may obtain both maternity leave and parental leave benefits. This means that a family by birth is entitled to a total of twenty-five weeks of unemployment insurance benefits while a family by adoption is entitled to only ten weeks of benefits.

Minimum Number of Weeks of Unpaid Leave

	Maternity[a]	Parental[b]	Adoption[c]
Federal Companies	17	24[d]	
Alberta	18		8[e]
British Columbia	18	12	
Manitoba	17	17	
New Brunswick	17	12[d,f]	
Newfoundland	17	12	17
Northwest Territories	17	12	
Nova Scotia	17	17	
Ontario	17	18	
Prince Edward Island	17	17	
Quebec[g]	18	34	
Saskatchewan	18	6[h]	6
Yukon Territory	17		

[a] Available to a mother by birth only.
[b] Unless otherwise stated, available to each parent, whether by birth or adoption.
[c] Unless otherwise stated, available to each adoptive parent.
[d] Available to *either* parent, whether by birth or adoption. Total family leave cannot exceed number stipulated.
[e] Available to *either* adoptive parent. Total family leave cannot exceed number stipulated.
[f] Called Child Care Leave not Parental Leave.
[g] Employees also entitled to a five-day birth or adoption leave—two of which may be paid.
[h] Paternity Leave—only available to a father by birth.

Yes, this is totally unfair. Families created by adoption are being denied the same amount of publicly-supported leave as families created by birth. Let's hope that by the time you are ready to claim your benefits, the few determined adoptive parents who are fighting this discrimination will have been successful.

One more point about unemployment insurance benefits. If the net income of the parent who receives the unemployment benefits is above a certain amount for the year, a portion of the benefits must be paid back. The repayment is calculated on the income tax return. For the 1993 tax year, the net income threshold was $58,110.

To find out more about claiming your benefit, contact your local Human Resources Development Canada office. Look under "Unemployment Insurance" in the government listings of your telephone directory.

Registering with the Government

There are two types of government registrations that should be dealt with when the child is placed in your home. First, your child will need a provincial health insurance number. Without this number, a doctor treating your child cannot be paid by the government. Obviously, something no doctor wants. If a health insurance number for your child is not relayed to you in the hospital, talk to your adoption professionals. They will either get a number for you or know the best route for you to obtain the number yourself.

You should also investigate the possibility of receiving child tax benefits. This benefit is a monthly cheque that replaces the family allowance parents once received. It is available to anyone providing care to one or more children with a combined family net income below a stipulated amount. The amount varies depending on how many children are receiving care and changes yearly. For the 1993 tax year, the maximum family net income with respect to one child was $70,000. Call 1-800-387-1193 to obtain an application form and further information.

Generally, you cannot obtain a birth certificate for your child until the adoption order is issued. After the order is issued, the birth records are changed to reflect the adoptive family's name. You can then complete an ordinary request form with the appropriate provincial office (look up "Birth Certificates" in the government pages in your telephone book).

Unfortunately, without that birth certificate, you cannot obtain a passport for your child or have your child added to your passport. Therefore, talk to your adoption professional, well before any planned travel, about getting an official letter that gives you permission to cross international borders with your child.

Obtaining Information about the Adoption

After the adoption order for your child has been issued, the government adoption records will be sealed. However, there are usually procedures that allow information contained in the records to be released to your family as well as the birth family.

Obtaining information that gives general background but does not identify any individuals—*non-identifying information*—is generally a simple process. Some provinces do, however, require an *acceptable* reason for the request. What will be considered acceptable varies.

For an adoptee, non-identifying information might include, for example, birth parents' ethnic background, level of education, type of occupation, religious affiliation and interests. It might also contain the circumstances that led to the adoption and a medical history of the birth family.

It is likely that neither you nor your child will need to ask the government for this type of information, that you already have the details. With most adoptions completed today, the adoptive parents obtain non-identifying information during the adoption process, either directly from the birth parents or indirectly through adoption professionals.

In the past, adoption professionals felt that birth parents and adopted children needed *fresh starts*. Birth and adoptive families were kept apart; each was given little or no information about the other. As previously discussed, it is now recognized that birth parents need to know details about their children's future and adoptees need to know about their past.

Depending on the openness of your child's adoption, your child may, in the future, need to contact the government to get desired *identifying information* about birth relatives. Obtaining such information is currently difficult. Unless there is a medical emergency, most provinces only allow identifying information to be revealed with the consent of both parties.

The system most often used is a *disclosure* or *reunion registry*. Adult adoptees add their names to the registry when they want to find their birth relatives. Similarly, birth relatives register when they want to find an adopted relative. When there is a match, identifying information is disclosed. Sometimes, counselling is available or required before the release of the information.

When an adoptee registers and no matching birth relatives are found, some provinces will conduct a search. Birth relatives listed in the adoption records are contacted and informed of the request for information made by their adopted relative. The birth relatives may then decide whether they want to register so that identifying information may be exchanged.

In the past few years there has been much lobbying by adoptee organizations to open the adoption records. They are concerned about the long wait that often occurs when an adoptee asks their government to search for birth relatives. In addition, many adoptees argue that they have the right to know their background, to know about their birth family. They feel that no one, neither the government nor their birth family, has the right to deny them that information.

One cannot predict what the future will provide for your child. However, there is a definite trend towards openness. For example, Ontario recently decided to provide requesting adult adoptees with an unaltered copy of their adoption order. The order states an adoptee's pre-adoption name and, usually, the name of the birth mother.

Raising Your Adopted Child

This book is almost finished. You have your child; you are ready to be a parent. Do not, however, forget what you have learned: parenting by adoption is different.

It was only a short time ago that adoption professionals claimed there was no difference. Adoptive parents were encouraged to pretend that their child was theirs by birth. The adoption was hidden from everyone, even the child. Yet, inevitably, the adoptee discovered the truth. With that discovery came much pain. The adoptee's sense of self was thrown into turmoil. Relationships were often irrevocably damaged.

Sensibly, professionals began advising adoptive parents to tell their child about the adoption. Yet, some families created by adoption still had difficulty. Many adoptive parents felt uncomfortable discussing the adoption, often, because they wanted to protect their child and themselves from any pain. Adoptees sensed this uneasiness and shied away from discussing the issues that concerned them.

In his 1964 book, *Shared Fate*,[1] Canadian sociologist H. David Kirk introduced the theories that are accepted today. An adoptive family is different from a biological family. The lines of communication about the adoption and the resulting differences must be kept open.

This does not mean that adoption should be a constant topic of conversation. However, you need to understand the differences and be prepared to deal with the resulting issues when they arise.

There are several books that can help. A few were mentioned in Chapter 1: Lois Melina's *Raising Adopted Children: A Manual for Adoptive Parents*, Judith Schaffer and Christina Lindstrom's *How to Raise an Adopted Child*, or Stephanie Siegel's *Parenting Your Adopted Child: A Complete and Loving Guide*. Lois Melina, thought to be the guru in this area by many adoptive parents, has also written *Making Sense of Adoption*[2] and produces the monthly newsletter *Adopted Child* (see Appendix II for contact information).

You should also continue your involvement with the adoptive parent support groups and adoption organizations you joined to find your child. These groups and organizations can provide invaluable assistance in the years to come. You will have the opportunity to talk to parents of children who are going through, or have survived, the stages being visited by your child. Your child will have friends who, just like her, joined their families by adoption. In addition, you will become part of the adoption community—staying abreast of the latest in adoption issues. The people you meet and the knowledge you gain will be invaluable, both for parenting and when it's time for another addition to your family.

That's it. No more concerns; no more advice. Well, just a little more advice. If you have not yet found your child, do not give up hope. There are so many options. Keep trying. It is worth the pain and effort. If you have found your child, it's time to relax and enjoy. Good luck.

Endnotes

[1] Kirk, H. David. *Shared Fate: A Theory and Method of Adoptive Relationships*. Brentwood Bay, B.C.: Ben-Simon Publishers, 1964, 1984.
[2] Melina, Lois Ruskai. *Making Sense of Adoption: A Parent's Guide*. New York: Harper & Row Publishers, 1989.

Tears for My Son

I sometimes cry when I think of my son. Tears that start as a spasm in my stomach and then suddenly run down my cheek. Tears that I hide lest they are misunderstood.

Often they are tears of fear. They pour from somewhere deep inside when I hear the horrors that have been inflicted on another's child—horrors that could have been inflicted on my child.

Pleasant are the tears of joy. The quiet tears that flow from a happy ending to a scary story. The little boy found unharmed after wandering lost in the snow. The man who manages to hold onto his grandson as someone tries to grab him away.

Tears follow my voice raised in anger. I am always sure I could have handled his misbehaviour in a better way. Yet I know I am a good mother. Everyone says I am a good mother, so it must be true.

At times I feel a wave of emotion so strong that tears are needed to relieve the growing pressure. He may have just given me a spontaneous hug or looked at me with that mischievous grin. He may be fast asleep on his back with his arms spread out wide—content, trusting, open to everything the world has to offer.

Then there are the tears I do not understand. They can occur at any time. Sometimes they leave me feeling curiously content; sometimes it is melancholy which lingers. I can never quite grasp their meaning. All I know is that thoughts of my son are at their core.

He is my first, my only, child. His birth changed me—deepened my emotions. There was suddenly someone other than myself to consider, to protect. Overnight, the world was different; its horrors and joys somehow closer.

All new parents must feel this change. The frequency of their tears must surprise them. Yet do they also have tears that they do not understand? Tears that seem to flow for no reason. Or does the answer lie not in parenthood but in how I became a parent. □

I was not at the birth of my son. He was five hours old when I met him. Sometimes I wonder about those hours I missed. What were his first thoughts as he entered his new world? Did he cry out? Did he greedily gulp the air that filled his lungs? Did he sense that the people who would most shape his life were not near, did not yet know he had taken that first breath?

I wonder if he was held. I mean really held—not simply laid in someone's arms but snuggled at a breast where he could hear a heart beat and feel comfort. I wonder if Debbie held him—Debbie, the woman who gave birth to my son.

Before I met Debbie, she was simply *her*. We had talked on the phone but she was not yet real. She was this voice that had control over our happiness, our lives. Every word she uttered caused my husband and me to either ascend into a blissful trance or swirl back down into despair. We were so scared—scared we would not like her, scared she would not like us, scared it would all fall apart.

The meeting was wonderful. She was wonderful—warm, caring and intelligent. Her parents were so supportive. I could not believe it; they too were scared.

Debbie thanked us. *She* thanked *us*. She said that she no longer felt like she was giving us her child but that she was giving her child a family. All the air seeped out of my chest. I let myself hope, just a little, that our years of trying, waiting and hoping might soon be over.

Caution was easy—this time. Yes, there was another time. That time, our excitement overwhelmed us. The clues that warned us over and over ''Hold back, Shane is going to change her mind'' are now obvious. But at the time, we thought everything was perfect.

Shane went into labour on Tuesday. Wednesday morning, she gave birth to an eight-pound six-ounce boy. Wednesday afternoon, she told her social worker that she didn't want us to come to the hospital just yet. On Saturday, she left the hospital with the baby.

We were nervously excited on Tuesday, ecstatic by Wednesday morning, worried but hopeful Wednesday afternoon. Saturday, and Sunday and Monday, I spent in bed.

Our ordeal was not over. We had made the mistake of sharing our excitement with family and good friends. We now had to share our pain. I remember having to console a devastated friend.

November 20, 1991. A date I will never forget. I wonder what he is like. I hope he is happy.

By the time we met Shane, we had been on the medical make-a-baby treadmill for almost three years. Three years—a short period for this sort of thing—of physical and emotional hell. That first December, I wrote my own version of the ''Twelve Days of Christmas.'' Every day of treatment my doctor brought to me: three self-inflicted needles, two bruising blood tests and an ultrasound by a novice nurse.

Each attempt was the one that was going to work. Each failure was worse than the one before. Weeks of praying for the right result followed weeks of treatment followed weeks of recovering from the previous attempt.

Our relationships with family and friends suffered. We felt isolated. They felt uncomfortable.

They were never sure if they should invite us to their kids' birthday parties.

They hesitated before telling us that they were once again pregnant. We were quick to say that we wanted to share those moments, that we were happy for them. Yet they knew that sometimes, just sometimes, we also felt a little sorry for ourselves.

One day, it was enough. Actually, there were months of slowly sinking spirits before I finally broke down and said: "I cannot go on . . . we must move on."

Moving on. For us, that meant adoption. The *childfree lifestyle* was not an acceptable alternative.

I was excited when I made that first phone call to the public adoption agency. We were finally strong enough to walk out of the casino. That's what it was like. We were gamblers who kept placing money and hope in a slot-machine, sure that the next pull was going to find the right combination. Afraid to stop lest we miss the jackpot.

A seven-year wait. That is what I was told. Seven more years.

Tears flowed that day. Understandable, recognizable tears— tears of despair and frustration.

A few sleepless nights. Then someone mentioned "private adoption." Like anyone who reads the newspaper, we had heard about it. But we didn't really understand what it meant.

A friend arranged for us to talk to a couple she knew who had adopted a child. They told us their story and then arranged for us to meet another couple. We were amazed at the compassion of virtual strangers. They shared their sorrows and joys with us, simply because they, too, had been through this hell.

We learned that we need not sit and wait. We learned that we could fulfil our dream by finding a pregnant woman who wanted us to adopt her unborn child. The harder we worked at letting people know we were looking, the greater our chances of success. Unbelievable, a process which allowed us to regain some control over our lives. We were hooked.

Private adoption—not an illegal or unethical adoption, but simply an adoption that is not arranged by the government. *Not arranged by the government* does not mean *do whatever you want*. Provincial laws must still be met. Laws which attempt to protect all of the parties involved: the adopted child, the biological parents and the adoptive parents.

We told everyone we were trying to adopt—every friend, acquaintance, business associate, shopkeeper, hairdresser, taxi-driver. . . . We wrote every doctor we or our friends or our friends' friends knew. We worked tirelessly for months and months and months until finally we received a phone call from someone who knew someone who knew Shane.

After Shane changed her mind, we decided to wait a little while before restarting our efforts. We couldn't muster the necessary enthusiasm. We needed time to heal. A month passed. Then, on Christmas Eve, a card from a stranger brought us more than season's greetings.

Debbie was six months' pregnant. For reasons that are hers to tell, she felt she could not raise her unborn child. She knew that with a private adoption, she could meet and choose the adoptive parents. She had heard our story. She wanted to meet us.

Having survived our ride on the medical treadmill, we thought we would have very little problem dealing with the stress inherent in the adoption process. Were we wrong.

I left our meeting with Debbie literally jumping with joy. In my hands was a teddy bear, a gift from Debbie for our unborn child. That night, my husband and I were so excited that we lay in bed talking until early morning. As exhaustion took over and the room became quiet, it suddenly hit me: there was nothing more for us to do.

Years of medically pursuing our child. Months of spreading the word about our desire to adopt. Weeks on an emotional roller-coaster before actually meeting Debbie. Everything had suddenly stopped. There was nothing for us to do, nothing to keep us busy. All we had to do was wait for the birth of our child. Simple. Just wait. Ha.

First there was the ever gnawing fear. The fear that Debbie, like Shane, would change her mind. Debbie had assured us that she knew adoption was best for her and her unborn child. But so had Shane. They were not trying to increase our pain. They were simply young women going through the most difficult time in their lives.

Somewhere along the way, we had become fatalists. We believed that our child was out there, waiting for us. Our child was not Shane's child. We hoped Debbie's child was our child. But if not . . .

This attitude was necessary and helpful but it didn't stop the fear. It simply let us know that we would survive, even if our hopes for this child did not.

There was also the isolation from the pregnancy. We had nothing to connect us to the approaching birth. My body was not changing. I wanted to feel my child kick. I wanted to hear a beating heart, to see a fuzzy shape. I even wanted to be sick. I wanted to be Debbie.

As Debbie's due date drew near, our state of panic became more acute and obvious. We had held off as long as we could before telling our parents. We had yet to tell any friends or our siblings. Trying to spare ourselves any extra pain, should the worst happen, we shamelessly lied when asked what was going on.

I stopped doing anything, going anywhere. I borrowed a cellular phone and carried it anytime I left the house. Every time the phone rang, I would forget to breathe. My mouth would go dry. I would have trouble saying hello. If it wasn't the social worker handling our adoption, I would quickly free the line. When the phone hadn't rung in over fifteen minutes, I would check to make sure it was working.

When the call finally came, it was Debbie and not the social worker. "You have a son" are the most beautiful words I have ever heard.

Knowing that it was the right thing to do and yet desperately wanting to run to the nursery, we first went to visit Debbie. Her parents by her side, she sweetly told us a little about the birth. At the time, it seemed like too many words. Now, we wish she had told us more. She then told us to go visit our son.

What can one say to describe the feeling as you look for the first time at your child? Wonder. Awe. He was so small, so beautiful. He didn't feel like he was mine. I felt like someone might at any moment scream: "What are you doing? Put him down." I wasn't worried, I knew it would not take long before everything felt right. It didn't.

Suddenly, we were unequipped parents. We had spent all of our energy trying to find him. Now that we had him, we didn't know what to do with him. Never wanting to raise my hopes any higher than they already were, I had prevented myself from doing much reading. Not that it would have been much help in those first few days.

We set up camp in the nursery. We arrived at dawn and didn't leave until we were exhausted. The nurses were wonderful. They showed us how to care for him. We quickly became, if not proficient, able.

Our anxieties were not over. Debbie still had to leave the hospital without him, sign a consent to adoption a few days later and then let twenty-one days go by without changing her mind.

There were nervous moments. Debbie coming back to hug him once more after she had already said goodbye and left the hospital. Her calling us a few days later. We were always outwardly calm. Yet she sensed our anxieties and tried hard, through her pain, to reassure us.

It had been our plan to go into hibernation for the twenty-one-day period during which she could change her mind. It just wasn't practical. In any event, we were too excited. Our son was coming home. We called our siblings and good friends with the news. All of the pain getting to this moment was washed away by our laughter and tears.

The twenty-one-day period was not as bad as we thought it would be. Do not misunderstand me. The day it ended, a cloud lifted from our lives. But we were too busy being new parents to become overwhelmed with worry.

Debbie is not totally gone from our lives. We send her pictures and notes, letting her know how and what he is doing. She sends him birthday and Christmas cards. Part of me would like her to simply disappear—the selfish, "I don't want to share him" part. The rest of me understands she is not a threat to our relationship.

I am his mommy. It is me he calls when he wakes up in the middle of the night. Me he runs to when he is hurt or wants a hug. Someday, it will be important for him to know who she is, to understand how much she cares for him. □

So that is my story. Am I any closer to understanding the reason for those tears? I am not sure. I do know that the tears are not caused by the consequences of my infertility.

My son and I are not biologically related. So what? There is also no genetic connection with the other most important person in my life, my husband.

We would have wanted our child to have my husband's sense of humour and my nose. He would surely have had my sense of humour and my husband's nose. Since we have no expectations, there can be no disappointments, only excitement at the possibilities. Two tone-deaf parents may even have a musically gifted son.

Our son is a joint effort—from the moment he was first imagined, through finding and caring for him, to helping him learn to take care of himself. No one could convince me that I do not have a child conceived with my chosen life partner.

I would have liked to experience a *normal* pregnancy and birth. At least, I think I would. Yet, we did have our own child creating experiences. Someone once said that the process of adopting was "the longest labour on record." The difficulty of our labour brought us closer. It made us realize the strength of our commitment to each other and to having a family.

I would not change anything that led me here. Because, you see, he is my son. It is so much more than the simple idea that I could not love a child any more than I love him. No one else could be my son. I am glad I cannot have a biological child, glad the public adoption agency was unhelpful, glad Shane changed her mind. If any of those events had not happened, my son would not be my son. Unimaginable.

So why do I cry those tears? I still don't know. But I now realize that I just don't care. It is contentment and not melancholy which most often lingers. I am probably thinking too much. In any event, I am too happy to care. Let the tears come.

* * *

Appendices

appendix · · · · · · · · · · · · · · · · · I

Adoptive Parent Support Groups and Adoption Organizations

New groups and organizations are constantly being formed. Existing groups and organizations sometimes quietly fold. Contacts change. We apologize for any inconveniences caused by out-of-date information. Please help us make future additions as current as possible. Send information about your group or organization to:

Judith Wine
Canadian Adoption Guide
c/o McGraw-Hill Ryerson
Professional and Consumer Division
300 Water Street
Whitby, Ontario L1N 9B6

Also included in this appendix is information on Infertility Support Groups and Organizations.

National

Adoption Council of Canada / Conseil d'adoption
 du Canada
Box 8442, Stn. T
Ottawa, Ont. K1G 3H8
613-446-4144; FAX: 613-788-5075

Infertility Awareness Association of Canada
 (IAAC)
523-774 Echo Drive
Ottawa, Ont. K1S 5N8
613-730-1322 or 1-800-263-2929; FAX:
 613-730-1323

Alberta

Provincial Organization

Adoptive Parents Assn of Alberta
Box 6496
Bonneyville, Alberta T9N 2H1
403-826-5625

Specific-focus Support Groups and Organizations

Endometriosis Assn, Edmonton Chapter
contact: Maureen Hill 456-6899

Support for families adopting Romanian
   children
415 Willowgrove Cres SE
Calgary Alta. T2J 1N5
contact: Denise MacDonald 271-9303

Support for families adopting Romanian
   children
RR 3
South Edmonton, Alta. T6H 4N7
contact: Mr Loren Stark 955-7774

T.A.D.A.
11803 78 Ave
Edmonton, Alta. T6G 0N8
For parents of hyperactive or attention-deficit
   children

North East Adoption Resources (NEAR)
General Delivery
Elk Point, Alta. T0A 1A0
contact: Marie Ibach 724-2216
Support group for special-needs adoptive
   parents

Families of Native Children
Box 15, Site 1, RR 2
Leduc, Alta. T9E 2X2
contacts: Fran Wolver 437-1287, Linda
   Long/Peter Portlock 469-4047

Support for Non-Native Parents with Native
   Kids
contact: Lorraine 241-9181

Families of Black Children
contacts: Sue 467-0934, Shelagh 986-8731

Edmonton Adopting Beyond Infancy
   Association
Adoption Support Line
contact: Andrea 461-2142

Adoption Options' Adoptive Parents Support
   Group
#30 7340—78 St
Edmonton, Alta. T6C 2N1
contact: Marilyn Shinyei 465-1238
For clients of the agency Adoption Options

Endometriosis Assn, Edmonton Chapter
contact: Maureen Hill 456-6899

General-focus Support Groups and Organizations

NORTHERN ALBERTA

North East Adoption Resources (NEAR)
Fort McMurray contacts: Tara and Dick
   Nelson 743-8044

South Peace Adoptive Parents Assn
Grande Prairie area
contacts: Clara Bryce 538-2385, Helen
   Cronkite 538-5477

Grizzly Trail Adoptive Families Assn
contacts: Dee Krysa 674-3602, Ann Pipe
   674-8204

North Peace Adoptive Support Group
Box 63
High Level, Alta. T0H 1Z0
contact: Debbie Delisle

Lesser Slave Adoptions Network
High Prairie area
contacts: Penny Roberts 523-2496, Brenda
   Perry 523-2173, Norm Goodwin
   523-6650

North East Adoption Resources (NEAR)
Box 1085
Lac La Biche, Alta. T0A 2C0
contact: Lori Thompson 623-3265
NACAC provincial representative

Adoptive Parents Assn of Alberta, Lakelands Chapter
contacts: Helen Jansen 826-2078, Carol Morton 826-5625

Lakeland Adoptive Parents Assn
Box 1119
Medley, Alta. T0A 2M0

Peace Adoptive Parents Assn
contact: Sharon Bloom 835-4848

Peace River Area Adoption Support Group
contact: Lynn King and Sharon Pountney 624-6460

North East Adoption Resources (NEAR)
Westlock contact: Garry Kearns 349-5280

CENTRAL ALBERTA

Adoptive Parents Assn of Alberta, Edmonton Chapter
contact: Sandy Plante 467-0322

North East Adoption Resources (NEAR)
Lloydminster contact: Bill Braun 871-6406

Lougheed Support Group
contact: Ed and Darlene Albecht 888-2124

Adoptive Parents Assn of Alberta, Marwayne Chapter
contacts: Lillian Reimer 847-2472, Penny Ford 847-3949

Adoptive Parents Assn of Alberta, Red Deer Chapter
contact: Judith Hathaway 343-8152

Red Deer and Area Support Group
contacts: Robin 347-8114, Jean 346-6883

Hinton Edson Grande Cache Support Groups
Box 36, Site 8, RR2
Stony Plain, Alta. T0E 2G0
contact: Garth Tylor-Meher 963-5727

North East Adoption Resources (NEAR)
Vermilion contact: Debbie 853-2363

SOUTHERN ALBERTA

Adoptive Parents Assn of Alberta, Calgary Chapter
contact: Margaret Ramsay 225-0145

Calgary Adoption Resource Foundation (CARF)
1020 Lake Ontario Dr SE
Calgary, Alta. T2J 3K2
contact: Kimm Reneau 276-9907

Hanna Support Group
contact: Linda Ford 326-2177

Medicine Hat Adoptive Support Group
Box 187
Irvine, Alta. T0J 1V0
contact: Gitti Weisner 529-1723

Adoptive Parents Assn of Alberta, Lethbridge Chapter
contact: Eric Kokko 327-7001 or 327-7774

Lethbridge Adoptive Parents Support Group
1229 7th Ave S
Lethbridge, Alta. T1J 1K6
contact: David Heatherington 329-1997

South Eastern Post Adoption Support Society
c/o Community Resources Centre
631 Prospect Dr SW
Medicine Hat, Alta. T1A 4C2
529-8916

Olds/Didsbury Adoption Support Group
Box 995
Sundre, Alta. T0M 1X0
contact: Karen and Doug Creelman 638-4873

British Columbia

Provincial Organizations

Adoptive Parents Assn of British Columbia
Suite 205, 15463-104th Ave
Surrey, B.C. V3R 1N9
604-588-7300 or 588-6111, FAX: 588-1388

Society of Special Needs Adoptive Parents
409 Granville St., Suite 1150
Vancouver B.C. V6C 1T2
604-687-3114 or toll-free 800-663-7627, FAX: 687-3364

Specific-focus Support Groups and Organizations

Society of Special Needs Adoptive Parents:
Coquitlam/Maple Ridge Area Group contact:
Rick 465-7056

North Vancouver Area Group contact: Dave
980-6837

Prince George Area Group contact: Rye
964-6299

Richmond/Vancouver Area Group contact:
Donna 525-5069

Surrey Area Group #1 contact: Jan
589-2751

Surrey Area Group #2 contact: Helen
597-1760

Single Adoptive Parents Support Group
4032 Coast Meridian Rd.
Port Coquitlam, B.C. V3B 3P4
contact: Lois B Reimer 941-5144

Romanian Orphans Support Group
Box 3392
Langley, B.C. V3A 4R7
contact: Sonya Paterson 534-5395

Romanian Adoptive Families Support Group
14664 Bellevue Cresc
White Rock B.C. V4B 2V2
White Rock contact: Rebecca Kennedy
531-0909
Nanaimo contact: Margo Sterling-Laycock
248-5013

Adoptive Families of Native Children
Suite 205 15463-104th Ave
Surrey, B.C. V3R 1N9
contacts: Trudy Denton 588-7300 (NACAC
provincial representative), Linda 272-5628

Haiti Adoptive Families
18085 60th Ave.
Surrey, B.C. V3S 1V5
contact: Diane Pernitsky 576-8308

Haitian Support Group
contact: Sandra Knopf 589-4490

Support Group for those with Afro-American
Children
contacts: Yvonne Devitt 591-7200, Karen
Madeiros 464-9944

Peruvian Adoptive Families
contact: Elsa Weinstein 876-4543

Vancouver Infertility Peer Support Group (VIP)
18131—57th Avenue
Cloverdale, B.C. V3S 5N1
contact: Jennifer Hillman 576-0037

Canadian Pelvic Inflammatory Disease Society
contact: Jill Weiss 684-5704

Endometriosis Assn, Vancouver Chapter
contact: Darlene Schleuter 943-4057

General-focus Support Groups and Organizations

UPPER MAINLAND

Adoptive Parents Assn of B.C.
  Fort Nelson Chapter contact: Cheryl
  Charters 774-2084

  Fraser Lake Chapter contact: Connie
  Neilson 699-6262

  Prince George Chapter contacts: Michelle
  Cote 964-2916, Lynda Shykora
  964-8151

  Prince Rupert Chapter contacts: Coreen
  Biech 627-1195, Paula Mojak 624-2949

  Terrace Chapter contacts: Marsha Lloyd
  635-5010, Lori Merrill 635-9533

LOWER MAINLAND

Adoptive Parents Assn of B.C.
  Abbotsford/Mission Chapter contacts:
  Louise Vis 856-5019, Jayne Forcier
  853-7466

  Chilliwack Chapter contacts: Judy Stusiak
  792-6672, Shirley Stanton 858-0175

Adoptive Parents Assn of B.C. (cont.)
Invermere Chapter contact: Janet
Sweetman 342-6765

Kamloops Chapter contacts: Jennifer Lewis
374-5743, Raye Youde 372-2373

Kelowna Chapter contacts: Cathy Taylor
763-8008, Susan Gulenchyn 763-3330

Kootenays Chapter contact: Loretta
Kazakoff 365-3770

Lower Mainland Chapter contacts: Joanne
Graham 433-1044, Louse Renaud
929-7309, Sarah Best 985-8521

Revelstoke Chapter contacts: Linda Balyx
837-2347, Phyllis Makarewicz
837-2244

Salmon Arm Chapter contact: Denis Hearn
838-0027

South Okanagan Chapter contacts: Jann
Bouthillier 494-1321, Michele Sine
493-8157

Ucluelet and Tofino Chapter: contact
provincial office for referral 588-7300

Vernon Chapter contacts: Pam Vilac
545-9809, Randi Patterman 542-0774

Williams Lake Chapter contact: Mary
LeBlanc 392-6835

Infant Adoption Committee Adopting Parents
Group of B.C.
9637 Timber Valley Rd
Delta, B.C. V4L 2E7

Mrs Kerry Lomax
RR 4
493 Stanley Cres
Kelowna, B.C. V1Y 7R3

Missing Pieces Through Adoption
Box 61526 Brookswood P.O.
Langley B.C. V3A 8C8
530-2160

Mrs Heather Pearce
Box 203
Nelson, B.C. V1L 5P9

VANCOUVER ISLAND

Adoptive Parents Assn of B.C., Campbell
River Chapter
contacts: Ann Almond 923-5468, Jane
Jepson 923-7537

Adoptive Parents Assn of B.C., Courtenay-
Comox Chapter
contacts: Lynn Bromilow 338-7164, Mary
Crowley 338-5758

Adoptive Parents Assn of B.C., Port Alberni
Chapter
contact: June Mosdell 723-7253

Adoptive Parents Assn of B.C., Nanaimo
Chapter
contacts: Carol Jenkins 756-3006, Linda
Kurtz 756-9919

Adopting Parents Group of B.C.
Hope Bay P.O.
North Pender Island, B.C. V0N 2M0
contact: Mrs Barbara Tallboy

Adoptive Parents Assn of B.C., Victoria
Chapter
contacts: Val Reynolds 598-2248, Terry
Kluytmans 656-9355

Arbutus Society for Children
contact: Susan Lees 721-6798
Adoption Support Program for the Victoria
area

Manitoba

Manitoba Adoptive Parents Assn
1423 5th St
Brandon, Man. R7A 3M8
contact: Mrs R Miller Western

Adoptive Parent Support Group of Western
Manitoba
c/o Child and Family Services of Western
Manitoba
340—9th Street
Brandon, Man. R7A 6C2
726-6030

Adoptive Parents Support Group of Eastern
   Manitoba
Box 175, RR 5
Winnipeg, Man. R2C 2Z2

Adoption Support Group
South Winnipeg Family Information Centre
Hastings School
R.3—95 Pulberry
Winnipeg, Man. R2M 3X5
contact: Kirsty Hexham 253-9250

Project Opikihiwawin
119 Sutherland Ave
Winnipeg, Man. R2W 3C9
contact: Verna McKay 947-3765 (NACAC
   provincial representative) A support group
   for non-Native families who have adopted
   Native children

Infertility Awareness Association of Canada,
   Winnipeg Chapter
P.O. Box 2547
Winnipeg, Man. R3C 4B3
contact: Gail Leknes 889-2789

New Brunswick

Moncton Adoptive Parents Assn (Association
   des Parents Adoptifs de Moncton)
Box 20102
Moncton, N.B. E1C 9M1
contact: Mrs. Marion Webb 386-4744
   (NACAC provincial representative)

Saint John Adoptive Parents Assn
236 McNamara Dr
Saint John, N.B. E2J 3L4
contact: Geoff Clark

Newfoundland

Adoptive Parents Assn of Newfoundland and
   Labrador
35 Creston Place
St John's, Nfld. A1E 5W2
contact: Doreen Westera 709-745-1201

Northwest Territories

There are no support groups in the Northwest
   Territories.
   For assistance contact the Adoption
   Council of Canada (see above) or a local
   office of the Department of Social
   Services (see Chapter 4 for contact
   information).

Nova Scotia

Provincial Organization

Adoptive Parents Assn of Nova Scotia
Box 2511 Stn M
Halifax, N.S. B3J 3N5
contact: Mary Miller 902-422-2087
NACAC provincial representative

Additional Support Groups and Organizations

Adoptive Parents Assn
30 Smallwood Ave
Dartmouth NS B2W 3R5
contact: Bob Greene

Atlantic Families for Children
RR 1
Orangeville, N.S. B0E 2K0
contact: Jodie Sanders

Support group for people adopting from
   Romania
contact: Glen Stevens 823-2093

Infertility Awareness Association of Canada,
   Halifax Chapter
60 Bayview Rd
Halifax, N.S. B3M 1N9
contact: Catherine Clute 443-0343.

Ontario

Provincial Organization

Adoption Council of Ontario
134 Clifton Rd
Toronto, Ont. M4T 2G6
416-482-0021

Specific-focus Support Groups and
   Organizations

Child Welfare League of America/Canada
180 Argyle Ave Suite 312
Ottawa, Ont. K2P 1B7
contact: Sandra Scarth 613-235-4412 fax
   788-5075

International Social Service Canada (ISS)
55 Parkdale Rd
Ottawa, Ont. K1Y 1E5
contact: Rita Marland 613-728-1226,
   725-0625
ISS is active in policy and legislation
   governing international adoption, and
   intervenes in cases of problem
   international adoption.

Latin American Adoptive Families (LAAF) in
   Canada
41 Sparkhill Ave
Toronto, Ont. M4K 1G4
contacts: Lynne Wilson Orr 416-461-7988,
   David Lee 416-485-2127, Karen Hodgson
   905-333-9274

LAAF Parent Support Group
3 Chapel Rd
Etobicoke, Ont. M8W 1G2
contact: Ruth Gibson Cook 416-252-7058

Support for Parents Adopting & Raising world
   Kids (SPARK)
421 Jane St
P.O. Box 25028
Toronto, Ont. M6S 5A1
contacts: membership—Patty Lester
   416-782-0268; Alison Pentland-Folk
   416-604-9610

Single Parent Adoption Support Group (SPA)
40 Riverdale Ave
Toronto, Ont. M4K 1C3
contact: Marie Artt 416-469-2424

Romanian Adoption Support Group
31 Cleveland Place
London, Ont. N5Z 4T5
contact: Betty Dubrick 519-649-7131

International Families
RR 2
Bewdley, Ont. K9H 5B2
contact: Mrs Elsie Board

Catholic Adoption Group
Catholic Children's Aid Society
26 Maitland St
Toronto, Ont. M4Y 1C6
416-925-6641
contact: Dan Buttenham 416-237-0297

Catholic Adoption Group
553 Coldstream Ave
Toronto, Ont. M6B 2K8
contact: Joe Fillipi

Assn of Parent Support Groups in Ontario
11 Nevada Ave
Willowdale, Ont. M2M 3N9

Simcoe Area Infertility Support Group
RR 2
Beeton, Ont. L9G 1A0
contact: Sandy Bartlett 905-729-2682

Hamilton Infertility Support Group
contact: Paula Cinba 905-527-7294

Kitchener / Waterloo Infertility Self-Help
   Group
Natural Family Planning
67 Spadina Rd W
Kitchener, Ont. N2M 1E8
contact: Ruth Forbes 519-742-3979

Niagara Peninsula Infertility Support Group
7 Gale Cres., #807
St. Catharines, Ont. L2R 7M8
contact: Ila McLachlan 905-687-9603

Infertility Awareness Association of Canada,
   Ottawa Chapter
57 Ruskin St
Ottawa, Ont. K1Y 4A8
contact: Kelly & Gord Rabjohn 613-233-9542

Infertility Awareness Association of Canada,
   Toronto Chapter
160 Pickering St
Toronto, Ont. M4E 3J7
contact: Diane Allen 416-691-3611, FAX:
   690-8015

Infertility Information in Durham
contact: Susan & Ian Masters 905-655-4833

Windsor Infertility Support Group
contact: Diane Matlock 519-972-4984

Endometriosis Assn
London Chapter contact: Joan Milroy
  519-473-3620
Toronto Chapter contact: Rosemarie Greene
  416-968-3717

General-focus Support Groups and Organizations

SOUTHEASTERN ONTARIO

Open Door Society of Northumberland
RR 4 Division Street N
Cobourg, Ont. K9A 4J7
contact: Mrs Merete Brooks 905-372-8772

Kingston Adoptive Parent Assn
215 Days Rd
Kingston, Ont. K7M 3R3
contact: Carolyn Hollett

Adoptive Parents' Consumers Group of
  Ottawa
Children's Aid Society of Ottawa-Carleton
1370 Bank St
Ottawa, Ont. K1H 7Y3
contact: Nancy Umbach or Fran McIninch
  613-733-0670

Open Door Society of Ottawa
P.O. Box 9141, Station T
Ottawa, Ont. K1G 3T8
contact: Lynda Inkster 613-837-3532

Children's Aid Society Adoption Support
  Group
721 Vinette St
Peterborough, Ont. K9H 7E9
contact: Betty Young-Stirling 705-743-9751

CENTRAL ONTARIO

Barrie Adoption Support Group
86 Parkside Dr
Barrie, Ont. L4N 1X1
contact: Phil Rimmer 705-721-4725

Parents Concerned with Adoption
RR2
Brampton, Ont. L6V 1A1
contact: Gina and Ray Osborne

Niagara Canadopt Support Group
23 Juliana Rd
Grimsby, Ont. L3M 4J4
contact: Mr & Mrs P McKillop 905-945-4606

CAS Adoptive Parent Group
Children's Aid Society of Hamilton-Wentworth
143 Wentworth St S
Hamilton, Ont. L8N 2Z1

Peel Post Adoption Support Group
Mississauga/Brampton Ont.
contact: Judy Weaver 905-452-9056

Adoptive Parent Group of York Region
Family and Children's Service of York Region
Box 358
Newmarket, Ont. L3Y 4X7
contact: Mrs Joyce Taylor

Adoptive Parents Assn of Halton
59 Chisholm St
Oakville, Ont. L6K 3H6
contact: Barb Croucher

Parents Concerned with Adoption
93–925 Bayly St
Pickering, Ont. L1W 1L4
contact: Trish and Terry Caverly
  905-839-1961

Parents of Adopted Children
69 Sanderson Cres
Richmond Hill, Ont. L4C 5L5
contact: Ms Shavie Fagan

Adoptive Parents Support Group of Niagara
24 Ramlee Rd
St. Catharines, Ont. L2M 2K5
contact: Partricia Richard 416-935-7492

Canadopt Niagara
RR 1
St. Catharines, Ont. L2R 6P7
contact: Barbara Healey

Niagara Adoptive Parents Assn
52 Cherie Rd
St. Catharines, Ont. L2M 6L7
contact: Mr and Mrs Ken Basarada

Niagara Adoptive Parent Assn
8 Ridgewood Rd
St. Catharines, Ont. L2R 3S3
contact: Mrs Gail Richardson

Niagara Family and Children's Services
Adoption Support Group
Box 516 311 Geneva St
St. Catharines, Ont. L2R 6W5
905-937-7731

Toronto Adoption Group
113 Oak Park Ave
Toronto, Ont. M4C 4M6
contact: Bev Nettleton 416-423-5194

Toronto Adoption Group
5 Bracken Ave
Toronto, Ont. M4E 1N1
contacts: Mrs Terry Condie
Alice Clinton 368-9791

Families in Adoption
134 Clifton Rd
Toronto, Ont. M4T 2G6
contact: Pat & Aaron Fenton 416-487-9938

SOUTHWESTERN ONTARIO

Gerry and Karen Bohr
73 Elizabeth St
Baden, Ont. N0B 1G0
519-634-5637

Brant Adoptive Parent Assn
15 Hawthorne Lane
Brantford, Ont. N3R 6R1
contact: Ms Gail Redmond

Adoptive Parents Together
25 Kanata Cres
Brantford, Ont. N3R 7E8
contact: Mrs C King

Informed Adoption
178 Cooper St
Cambridge, Ont. N3C 2N7
contact: Shirley Gibbs

Kent Adoptive Parent's Assn
264 Baldoon Rd
Chatham, Ont. N7L 1E6
contacts: Bob & Nancy Hillman
    519-354-0359; Mrs Joan Sass
    519-351-3209

Sharing Adoption
24 Hosking Place
Guelph, Ont. N1G 3R9
contacts: Mr and Mrs Noris 519-837-3998;
    Mr & Mrs R Bolten 519-824-8853

Post-Adoption Group
Family and Children's Service of Guelph &
    Wellington
55 Delhi St. Box 1088
Guelph, Ont. N1H 6N3
contact: R. Ceschan

Canadopt
RR 1
Ilderton, Ont. N0M 2A0
contact: Bob and Joan Cummings
    519-666-1224

Kincardine Canadopt
RR 5
Kincardine, Ont. N2Z 2X6
contact: Kathy Desmond 519-396-8737

Canadopt
RR 3
Komoka, Ont. N0L 1R0
contact: Mrs Donna Wolsey
    519-641-0796/2974 fax 519-641-2974

Nancy Pollard
873 Hellmuth Ave
London, Ont. N6A 3T9
519-439-7980

Perth County Adoptive Parent Assn
RR 5
Stratford, Ont. N5A 6S6
contact: Mrs Jean Anjema 519-393-6864

Waterloo Adoptive Parent Assn
529 Glenforest Blvd
Waterloo, Ont. N2L 4H9
contact: Fred & Marilyn Hovinga
    519-885-1647 or 824-8853

St. Clair Region Adoption Resource Centre
Box 2505 Walkerville Post Office
Windsor, Ont. N8Y 4S2
519-252-7487

CAS Post-Adoption Support Group
Essex Children's Aid Society
690 Catarqui St
Windsor, Ont. N9A 3P1
contact: Bev Thompson

Sharing Adoption Resource Group
Windsor, Ont.
contact: Mary Simonetto 519-944-3505

NORTHERN ONTARIO

Muskoka Adoptive Parent Assn
Box 2173
Bracebridge, Ont. P0B 1C0
Bracebridge contacts: Eric & Karen Kaye
    519-653-8917
Huntsville contacts: Joanne Lemke
    705-789-5865, Marlene 705-635-1654

Payukotayno, James and Hudson Bay Family
    Services
Box 336
Moosonee, Ont. P0L 1Y0
705-336-2229

Adoptive Parents Group
Children's Aid Society
Suite 300, 240 Algonquin Ave
North Bay, Ont. P1B 8K3
contact: Ron Lees or Eileen Larmer
    705-472-1910

Sault Ste Marie Canadopt
185 Panoramic Dr
Sault Ste Marie, Ont. P6B 6E3
contact: Ms Jennifer Smart 705-945-1170

Adoption Assn of Thunder Bay
Family and Children's Service of Thunder Bay
309 South Court St
Thunder Bay, Ont. P7B 2Y1

Adoptive Parent Group
Porcupine and District Children's Aid Society
12 Elm St N
Timmins, Ont. P4N 6A1
contact: Ms Anna Lisa Deluca 705-264-4257
    or 268-6655

AWARE
Box 265
Val Caron, Ont. P0M 3A0
contact: Evelyn Roberge-Pellerin
    705-897-6327

Prince Edward Island

West Prince Adoption Awareness and Support
    Group
O'Leary P.O., P.E.I. C0B 1V0
contacts: Rhonda Shaw 859-3257, Darlene
    Galant 859-2207

Montague Area Adoption Support Group
Dep't of Health and Social Services
Box 1500
Montague, P.E.I. C0A 1R0
contact: Marjorie Robertson, Resource
    Development Worker 838-2992

Adoptive Parents Support Group
Dep't of Health and Social Services
Box 2000
Charlottetown, P.E.I. C1A 7N8
contact: Richey Mayne, Resource
    Development Worker 368-5393

Quebec

Adoption Estrie
1517, rue Cyr
Fleurimont, Québec J1E 3B6
contact: Louise Chapdelaine 819-565-7986

Association des parents en adoption
    internationale du Saguenay-Lac St-Jean
4549, chemin St-André,
Jonquière, Québec G7X 7V4
contact: Michel Girard 418-542-7115

Adoption internationale démocratique pour
    enfant (A.I.D.E.)
6630 rue Vaudry
Laval, Québec H7B 1C6
contact: Edouard Amborski 514-661-1515

Association des Familles Québec-Chine
C.P. 146—Succ. Ahunstic
Montréal, Québec H3L 3N7
contact: Daniel Richard 514-856-3037

Fédération des parents adoptants du Québec
(F.P.A.Q.)
4264, rue Ferncrest
Pierrefonds, Québec H9H 2A1
contact: Claire-Marie Gagnon 514-696-0508

Association des parents pour l'adoption
internationale
C.P. 111
St-Jérôme, Québec J7Z 5T7
contact: Nicole Desjardins 514-431-1514

Présidente Association des parents des
enfants du monde (A.P.E.M.)
C.P. 1432
Trois-Rivières, Québec G9A 5L2
contact: Lucie Gamache 819-373-4096

Association Québécoise pour la Fertilité Inc.
8000, boul Langelier, Suite 804
Saint-Léonard, Québec H1P 3K7.
contact: Huguette Nadeau 514-445-8891,
Violaine Fortin 514-464-1857.

Saskatchewan

Provincial Organization

Saskatchewan Adoptive Parents Assn (SAPA)
210-2002 Quebec Ave
Saskatoon, Sask. S7K 1W4
306-665-7272

Additional Support Groups and Organizations

Saskatchewan Adoptive Parents Assn,
Moose Jaw Chapter
contact: Joanne Yuke 694-1627

Support Group for Parents of Transculturally
Adopted Adolescents contact: Bonnie
Young, Child and Youth Services, Regina
787-3400

Adoptive Parents of South Saskatchewan Inc
Box 252
Rouleau, Sask. S0G 4H0
contact: Ms. Randy Johner 776-2371

Swift Current Pre- and Post-Adoptive Parents
Group
contact: Glenna Dietrich 773-6973

Saskatchewan Infertility Support Group
contact: Roberta 966-8623

Yukon Territory

There are no support groups in the Yukon
Territory. For assistance contact the
Adoption Council of Canada (see above)
or a local office of the Department of
Health and Social Services (see Chapter 4
for contact information).

United States—Selected Groups and Organizations

North American Council on Adoptable
Children (NACAC)
970 Raymond Avenue, Suite 106
St. Paul MN 55114-1149
612-644-3036
An organization committed to meeting the
needs of waiting children in the U.S. and
Canada.

Adoptive Families of America (AFA)
3333 Highway 100 North
Minneapolis MN 55422
612-535-4829
Largest organization of adoptive families—
terrific source for books and tapes,
publishes *Adoptive Families* magazine (formerly *Ours Magazine*).

National Adoption Information Clearinghouse
(NAIC)
11426 Rockville Pike, Suite 410
Rockville MD 20852
301-231-6512; FAX: 301-984-8527
Provides access to information on all aspects
of adoption.

Resolve Inc.
1310 Broadway
Somerville MA 02144-1731
617-623-0744
A network of 54 chapters offering
information, referral, support and
advocacy services to infertile people.

**Much of the information set out in this
appendix was supplied by the newsletter
Adoption Helper (see Appendix II for contact
information).**

Adoption Newsletters and Magazines

We apologize for any inconveniences caused by out-of-date information. Please help us make future additions as current as possible. Send information about your newsletter or magazine to:

Judith Wine
Canadian Adoption Guide
c/o McGraw-Hill Ryerson
Professional and Consumer Division
300 Water Street
Whitby, Ontario L1N 9B6

Canadian Publications

Adoption Circles
Forget Me Not Family Society
Box 61526, Brookswood P.O.
Langley, B.C. V3A 8C8
Tel/FAX: 604-530-2160
4/yr, 12 pgs, $24/yr
"Canada's post-adoption quarterly" for adoptees, adoptive parents, birth parents and concerned professionals.

Adoption Helper
Katherin Jones, Editor
Robin R. Hilborn, Publisher
189 Springdale Blvd
Toronto, Ont. M4C 1Z6
Tel/FAX: 416-463-9412

Quarterly, 24 pgs, $28/yr in Canada, US$28/yr in the U.S., US$35/yr overseas, circ. 700, ISSN 1181-845X.

Adoption Roundup
Adoption Council of Ontario (ACO)
134 Clifton Rd
Toronto, Ont. M4T 2G6
416-482-0021; FAX: 484-7454
4/yr, 16 pgs, $25/yr ($50/yr for agencies), includes ACO membership.

Adoptive Parents Assn. of Alberta (APAA) Newsletter
361 Belvedere Heights West, 23109 Twp. Rd. 514
Sherwood Park, Alta. T8B 1K9
Quarterly, 32 pgs, $20/yr, includes APAA membership.

*Adoptive Parents Assn. of Nova Scotia
(APANS) Newsletter*
Box 2511, Stn. M
Halifax, N.S. B3J 3N5
902-422-2087
16 pgs, $15/yr, includes APANS membership.

Bulletin Fertilité (Fertility Newsletter)
Association Québécoise pour la Fertilité Inc.
8,000, boul. Langelier, Suite 804
Saint-Léonard (Québec) H1P 3K7
contact: Huguette Nadeau 514-445-8891 or
 Violaine Fortin 514-464-1857
Quarterly, 4 pgs, $30/yr includes
 membership. Text in English and French.
 Winter 1991 topic was adoption.

Canadopt Newsletter
Canadopt
RR 1
Ilderton, Ont. N0M 2A0
3/yr, 28 pgs, $20/yr, includes Canadopt
 membership.
contact: Joan Cummings

CRCL Linkletter
Canadian Romanian Children's Link (CRCL)
Box 94502, Thornhill East P.O.
2900 Steeles Ave East
Thornhill, Ont. L3T 7R5
416-969-0585
6/yr, 4 pgs, donation includes membership in
 CRCL, a charity helping children in
 Romanian orphanages.

Families for Children Newsletter
Families for Children
45 Russell Hill Rd
Toronto, Ont. M4V 2S9
contact: Mrs. Sandra Simpson 416-967-7148
 (Saturday only) or 514-967-6494 in
 Montreal
Newsletter for clients of agency

Families for Children Newsletter No. 2
Debbie Schmidt, Publisher
35195 Ewert Ave
Mission, B.C. V2V 6S7
Forum for adoptive families.

FPAQ Newsletter
Fédération des Parents adoptants du Québec
121 Biron
Drummondville (Québec) J2C 2Y8
$60 per family membership.

IAFG Newsletter
International Adoption Families Group (IAFG)
1009—17 Ave SE
Calgary, Alta. T2G 1J6
contact: Linda Spiteri 403-262-2938, FAX
 244-0450
4/yr, 6 pgs, $25/yr.

Infertility Awareness
Infertility Awareness Association of Canada
 (IAAC)
523-774 Promenade Echo Dr
Ottawa, Ont. K1S 5N8
613-730-1322 or 1-800-263-2929; FAX:
 613-730-1323
5/yr, 18 pgs, $35/yr, includes membership in
 IAAC.

ISS Canada Newsletter
International Social Service Canada (ISS)
55 Parkdale Rd.
Ottawa, Ont. K1Y 1E5
contact: Rita Marland 613-728-1226,
 725-0625
6 pgs, $25/yr.
ISS is active in policy and legislation
 governing international adoption, and
 intervenes in cases of problem
 international adoption.

LAAF News
Latin American Adoptive Families (LAAF) in
 Canada
41 Sparkhill Ave
Toronto, Ont. M4K 1G4
contacts: Lynne Wilson Orr 416-461-7988,
 David Lee 416-485-2127, Karen Hodgson
 905-333-9274
Quarterly, 20 pgs, $40/yr, includes LAAF
 membership.

Moncton Adoptive Parents Assn. Newsletter
Box 20102
Moncton N.B. E1C 9M1
506-386-4744
Quarterly, 16 pgs, $15/yr includes
 membership.

Newsletter Bulletin
Adoption Council of Canada (ACC)
Box 8442, Stn. T
Ottawa, Ont. K1G 3H8
613-235-1566; FAX 788-5075
4/yr, 8 pgs, $25/yr includes ACC membership.

Nova Scotia Adoptive Parents Assn.
Newsletter
Box 2511, Stn. M
Halifax, N.S. B3J 3N5

ODS News
Open Door Society (ODS)
Box 9141, Stn. T
Ottawa, Ont. K1G 3T8
613-521-6587
4/yr, 10 pgs, $25/yr includes ODS
membership.

OLA Ninos Newsletter
Opportunities for Latin American Children
(OLA)
41 Sparkhall Ave
Toronto, Ont. M4K 1G4
4 pgs, registered charity.
contact: Ralph Orr 416-461-7988

Parent Finders (National Capital Region)
Newsletter
Box 5211, Stn. F.
Ottawa, Ont. K0A 3M0
contact: Anne McLaughlin

PFI Communiqué,
Parent Finders Inc. (PFI)
2279 Yonge St., Suite #11
Toronto, Ont. M4P 2C7.
416-486-8346
14 pgs, $15/yr, includes membership.
Aids adoptees seeking their origins and birth
parents researching their children; register
of names.

SAPA News
Saskatchewan Adoptive Parents Assn.
(SAPA)
210-2002 Quebec Ave
Saskatoon, Sask. S7K 1W4
306-665-7272
Bi-Monthly, 18 pgs, $20/yr, includes SAPA
membership.

Shattered Dreams
c/o Born to Love
21 Potsdam Rd, Unit 61
Downsview, Ont. M3N 1N3
contact: Cathy McDermid 416-663-7143
For people who have experienced miscarriage.

SPA Newsletter
Single Parent Adoption Support Group
847 Clancey Cres
Newmarket, Ont. L3Y 8H2
4 pgs, $20/yr
contact: Lynn Irwin 416-469-2424

Sparks
Support for Parents Adopting and Raising
World Kids
421 Jane St., Box 25028
Toronto, Ont. M6S 5A1
4/yr, 15 pgs, $20/yr, includes membership.
contact: Keith Price 416-604-9610.

Special Needs Adoptive Parents Newsletter
Society of Special Needs Adoptive Parents
(SNAP)
409 Granville St, Suite 1150
Vancouver, B.C. V6C 1T2
604-687-3114 or 1-800-663-7627; FAX:
687-3364
4/yr, 16 pgs, $15/yr, includes membership in
SNAP.

Update Adoption Options
Adoption Options
#30 7340—78 St
Edmonton, Alta. T6C 2N1
403-465-1238
12-page newsletter for clients of licensed
adoption agency.

Vancouver Infertility Peer Support (VIPS)
Group Newsletter
18131 – 57th Ave
Cloverdale, B.C. V3S 5N1.
4 pgs, $10/yr includes VIPS membership.
contact: Jennifer Hilman 604-576-0037.

Windows on Adoption
Adoptive Parents Assn. of British Columbia
(APABC)
Suite 205, 15463-104th Ave
Surrey, B.C. V3R 1N9

604-588-7300, 604-588-6111,
1-800-563-9565; FAX 604-588-1388
9/yr, 32 pgs, $24/yr, includes APABC
membership.

Selected American Publications

ACORN
Adopted Children of Romania Network
299 Oak St
Patchogue NY 11772
4/yr, 18 pgs, US$10.
contact: Karen LoGrippo 516-289-9274.

Add-Option
AASK America (Aid to Adoption of Special
  Kids)
657 Mission St, Suite 601
San Francisco CA 94105
1-800-23AASK1, 415-434-2275
Sources of U.S.-born, hard-to-place children.

Adoptalk
North American Council on Adoptable
  Children (NACAC)
970 Raymond Ave., Suite 106
St. Paul MN 55114-1149
612-644-3036; FAX:644-9848
4/yr, 20 pgs, US$30/yr, Can$35/yr, includes
  membership in NACAC, circ. 3,500, ISSN
  0273-6497.
NACAC is committed to meeting the needs of
  waiting children in the U.S. and Canada.

Adopted Child
Lois Melina, Editer & Publisher
Box 9362, 105 E. Second St
Moscow ID 83843
208-882-1794
Monthly, 4 pgs, US$22/yr, US$32/yr in
  Canada, circ. 3,419. ISSN 0745-3167.
Deals with issues unique to parenting adopted
  children. The Adopted Child Library sells
  back issues of the newsletter as well as
  audio cassettes and books by Lois Melina.

Adoption Advocates Newsletter
Christine Adamec, Editor
1921 Ohio St NE, Suite 2
Palm Bay FL 32907
407-724-0815
12/yr, 8 pp., US$30/yr.

Adoption Law Journal
American Academy of Adoption Attorneys
2009 N. 14th St, Suite 510
Arlington VA 22201
703-522-8800

Adoption Report
Child Welfare League of America
CN 94 300 Raritan Center Parkway
Edison NJ 08818
The Child Welfare League also publishes Child
  Welfare and Children's Monitor.

Adoption Today
Concerned Persons for Adoption (CPA)
Box 179
Whippany NJ 07981
914-651-7075
Monthly, 14 pgs, circ. 425, US$10/yr,
  US$12/yr in Canada.
Committee reports, adoption information,
  updates on legislation.

Adoptionsdreieck
William L. Gage, Editor
805 Alvarado Drive NE
Albuquerque, NM 87108
Adoption newsletter in German.

Adoptive Families Update
Search Institute
700 S. Third St, #210
Minneapolis MN 55415
1-800-888-7828. Free.

Adoptive Families
Adoptive Families of America, Inc. (AFA)
3333 Hwy 100 N., Suite 203
Minneapolis MN 55422
612-535-4829
6 issues/yr, 96 pgs, US$24/yr in the U.S.,
  US$34/yr in Canada, includes membership
  in AFA, circ. 15,000—largest adoption
  periodical, ISSN 0899-9333. Formerly
  called Ours Magazine.

AdoptNet
Sondra Neuburger, Editor
Box 50514
Palo Alto CA 94303-0514
415-949-4370
6 issues/yr, US$20/yr in the U.S., US$25/yr

In Canada, 48 pgs. ISSN 1046-6843.
"Magazine of Adoption Networking and
Support—Creating a better understanding
of adoptees, birth familes and adoptive
families."

American Journal of Adoption Reform
1139 Bal Harbor Blvd
Suite 184
Punta Gorda FL 33950
Bi-weekly. "A national forum for opinions
about adoption-related issues."

Attachments
Attachment Center at Evergreen
Box 2764
Evergreen CO 80439
contact: Gail Trenberth 303-674-1910
4 pgs, articles and information on
attachment. The Center conducts
workshops on attachment and adoption
and treats troubled children.

Buenas Noticias
Latin America Parents Assn. National Capital
Region
Box 4403
Silver Spring MD 20914-4403
301-431-3407
4/yr, 36 pgs, US$25/yr.

CAP Book
The Cap Book, Inc.
700 Exchange St
Rochester NY 14608
716-232-5110
Photos and descriptions of hundreds of U.S.
Children waiting for Adoptive Parents.
US$75 for one yr, includes two-volume
book and bi-weekly updates.

Chain of Life
Janine Baer, Editor
Box 8081
Berkeley CA 94707
8 pgs, 6/yr, US$15/yr., circ. 100, $2 +
SASE for sample copy.
Feminist newsletter on adoption reform, open
adoption, donor insemination, surrogacy,
lesbian and gay family issues; for same-
gender adopters.

Children's Voice
National Coalition to End Racism in America's
Child Care System
22075 Koths
Taylor MI 48180
contact: Carol Coccia 313-295-0257
Quarterly, US$10/yr, 4 pgs, circ. 1,000.
Fights racism in adoption practices.

Connections
Gail Walton, Editor
1407 East Miner St
Arlington Heights IL 60004
4/yr, US$14/yr.
For parents of children from the Indian
subcontinent.

Copihue
U.S. Chilean Adoptive Families
1801 Miller Ct
Lake Geneva WI 53147
3/yr, US$18/yr.
contact: John Morack

Cousins
Douglas Kim, Editor
Box 4460, Berkeley CA 94704
6/yr.
Newsletter for school-aged Korean-Americans,
adopted and non-adopted.

Dear P.O.P.A.
Parents of Peruvian Adoptees
RD 4, Box 4304
Glen Rock PA 17327
717-235-6359
6/yr, 18 pgs $15/yr.
contact: Judi Fisher

FACE Facts
Families Adopting Children Everywhere
(FACE)
Box 28058, Northwood Station
Baltimore MD 21239
contact: Carol Mowbray 301-239-4252
6/yr, circ. 1,900, US$20/yr includes FACE
membership.

Family Law Quarterly
American Bar Assn
750 North Lake Shore Dr
Chicago IL 60611.

Includes adoption-related articles. Fall 1991 issue includes article on the role of sexual orientation in adoptions.

Family Ties
Attachment Disorder Parents' Network (ADPN)
Box 18475
Boulder CO 80308
contact: Gail Trenberth 303-443-1446
4/yr, 4 pgs, US$8/yr, includes ADPN membership.

FOLK
Families of Latin Kids
Box 15537
Ann Arbor MI 48106
16 pgs, circ. 75, US$15/yr includes membership in FOLK.

FPA Bulletin
Families for Private Adoption (FPA)
Box 6375
Washington DC 20015
contact: Claire K. Beth 202-722-0338
Quarterly, circ. 400, includes FPA membership.

FYI
WAIF
67 Irving Place
New York NY 10003
contact: Gerald H. Cornez (212) 533-2558.
2/yr, free, circ. 3,000, WAIF was founded in 1955 by actress Jane Russell to promote adoption of children.

GAP Newsletter
Group of Adoptive Parents (GAP)
1055 Grayview Ct
Cincinnati OH 45224
contact: Bob Simpson 513-541-4166
30 pgs, reprints of adoption-related articles.

Geborener Deutscher
William L. Gage, Editor
805 Alvarado Drive NE
Albuquerque, NM 87108
Quarterly, 4 pgs, free, in English, for German-born adoptees and their birth/adoptive families; help in searching for birth relatives in Germany.

Growing in Friendship Together
Adoptive Families of Romanian Children
519 Justin Ave., #4
Glendale CA 91201
contact: Suzan Black 818-548-4451
3/yr, free.

Growing with FAS
Pamela Groupe Groves, Editor
7802 SE Taylor
Portland OR 97215
503-254-8129
6 pgs, 6 issues/yr, US$12/yr, circ. 500.
Help in raising adopted children with Fetal Alcohol Syndrome or Fetal Alcohol Effect.

Guatemalan North-American Families Newsletter
Anita Rapone, Editor
16 Woodcliff Dr
Plattsburgh NY 12901
518-8850
4/yr, US$12.
Network of Guatemalan adoptive families.

Harmony
c/o Effingham Daily News
Box 836
Effingham IL 62401
A newsletter for multiracial adoptive families.

International Concerns Committee for Children—Newsletter
International Concerns Committee for Children (ICCC)
911 Cypress Dr
Boulder CO 80303
303-494-8333.
4/yr, US$10/yr, 34 pgs
Covers international adoption and general child welfare issues; legislative news.
ICCC also publishes: ICCC—Child Listing Service, photos and descriptions of hard-to-place foreign-born children in the U.S.; Report on Foreign Adoption and Reunions.

Jewish Children's Adoption Network
Box 16544
Denver CO 80216-0544
303-573-8113
Computer registry of children needing Jewish homes and Jewish families interested in adopting such children.

LAAF Quarterly
Latin American Adoptive Families (LAAF)
40 Upland Rd
Duxbury MA 02332
contact: Marilyn Rowland 617-934-6756
Quarterly, 36 pgs, US$24/yr, includes LAAF
membership, includes section on LAAF in
Canada. In Canada, subscribe through
LAAF in Canada listed above.

Namaste Newsletter
Gail Walton, Editor
1417 E. Miner St
Arlington Heights IL 60004
312-255-8309
For families with children from the Indian subcontinent.

National Adoption Center News
National Adoption Center (NAC)
1500 Walnut St., Suite 701
Philadelphia PA 19102
contact: Carolyn Johnson 215-735-9410
2/yr, free, circ. 12,500.
NAC promotes adoption of special-needs
children.

National Adoption Directory
National Adoption Information Clearinghouse
(NAIC)
11426 Rockville Pike, Suite 410
Rockville MD 20852
301-231-6512; FAX: 301-984-8527
Periodic, US$18.50 plus shipping.
Lists agencies and support groups by state.
NAIC also publishes various fact sheets and
brochures—write for catalogue.

National Adoption Reports
National Council for Adoption (NCFA)
William L. Pierce1930 17th St., NW
Washington DC 20009-6207
202-328-1200; FAX 332-0935
4/yr, 8 pgs, US$50 includes membership and
Annual Report, circ. 1,700.
For those who have adopted or are
considering adopting.
NCFA also publishes: *Legal Notes*, on
adoption court cases; *Memo*, on
legislation; *Unmarried Parents Today*, on
pregnancy counselling; *NCFA Directory of
Member Agencies*; *Adoption Factbook*:

*U.S. Data, Issues, Regulations and
Resources.*

NY Singles Adopting Children
Andrea Troy, Editor
Box 472
Glen Oaks NY 11004
212-249-4645, 718-229-7240
Quarterly, 12 pgs, US$36/yr.

Open Record
Americans for Open Records (AmFOR)
Box 401
Palm Desert CA 92261
619-341-2619
Quarterly, 2 pgs, circ. 5,000, ISSN
1044-1956.
A civil liberties organization acting through
lobbying and lawsuits on behalf of
adoptees, adoptive parents and
birthparents. Birth relatives search
information.

Our Chosen Children from Romania
Box 401
Barre VT 05641
6/yr, US$20.
For adoptive families of Romanian children.

Our Romanian Children
Box 8313
Argonne
IL 60439-8313
6/yr, US$10/yr.
For families adopting Romanian children.

Ours, see *Adoptive Families*

PACT Press
PACT—An Adoption Alliance, Inc.
3315 Sacramento St., Suite 239
San Francisco CA 94118
contact: Becca Martinson 415-221-6957
4/yr, US$32/yr.
"News and opinion on everything that
touches adopted children of color."

Parents for Private Adoption Newsletter
Parents for Private Adoption (PPA)
202 Battell Bldg.
Middlebury VT 05753
contact: Margaret Hutchison-Betts
802-545-2492
Quarterly, circ. 250.

People Searching News
Box 22611
Fort Lauderdale FL 33335-2611
305-370-7100
"The only adoption search magazine in North
America."
(searching for birth relatives)

*Perinatal Addiction Research and Education
Update*
National Assn. for Perinatal Addiction
Research and Education
11 E. Hubbard St., Suite 200
Chicago IL 60611
312-329-2512
Fetal Alchohol Syndrome / Effect resource.

Que Tal
Latin America Parents Assn (LAPA-New York)
Box 72
Seaford NY 11783
contact: Ermine Bennette 718-236-8689
Periodic newsletter, US$20/yr, includes LAPA
membership, circ. 600.
LAPA aids those adopting from Latin America.

Quest
KinQuest Inc.
Box 873, Bowling Green Stn
New York NY 10274-0873
contact: Carol Komissaroff 212-826-5644
Quarterly, 4 pgs, US$14/yr
Kin-Quest is an adoption- and genealogy-
related computer bulletin board system;
tel. 718-627-0811, modem
718-998-6303; member of FidoNet.

Report on Foreign Adoption
International Concerns Committee for Children
(ICCC)
911 Cypress Dr
Boulder CO 80303
303-494-8333
Annual, US$20/yr, listing costs, waiting
periods and types of children available
from agencies for adoption in North
America

Romania Children's Connection Newsletter
Box 10180
Alexandria VA 22310
contact: Mary Thomas 703-548-3061

Roots and Wings
Cynthia V. Peck, Editor
Box 638
Chester NJ 07930
908-637-8828; FAX 637-8699
4/yr, 56 pgs, US$20/yr, ISSN 1050-6624.
Magazine for families touched by adoption.
Personal experience balanced with advice
from experts.

Roundtable
National Resource Center for Special Needs
Adoption (NRCSNA)
16,250 Northland Dr., Suite 120
Southfield MI 48075
313-475-8693

Single Mothers by Choice
Box 1642, Gracie Square Stn
New York NY 10028

Single Parents with Adopted Kids
Dannette Kaslow, Editor
4116 Washington Rd., #202
Kenosha WI 53144-1515
20 pgs, 6/yr, US$20, US$28 in Canada, circ.
150, ISSN 1049-930X.

Source List
Committee for Single Adoptive Parents
(CSAP)
Box 15084
Chevy Chase MD 20815
contact: Hope Marindin 202-966-6367.
Published in July of odd yrs, 35 pgs, US$18
includes CSAP membership and three
updates to Source List. Lists about 95
agencies that are sources of adoptable
children and accept unmarried applicants.
CSAP also publishes *Handbook for Single
Adoptive Parents*, 70 pgs, US$8.

Source
Search Institute
122 West Franklin, Suite 525
Minneapolis MN 55404
612-376-8955
4/yr.
Newsletter on issues facing children,
adolescents and families. Ongoing
adoption study report is free: ask for
Adoptive Families Update.

Spice Rack
Lynn Beard, Editor
604 Rollingwood Dr
Greensboro NC 27410
Adoptions from India. Has a four-day cultural reunion.

Star Tracks
Stars of David International Inc.
5231E Memorial Dr, #175
Stone Mountain GA 30083
Quarterly, circ. 700, US$8/yr in the U.S., US$11/yr outside, includes membership.
contact:: Janie Allen 201-272-3156.
Support network for Jewish and part-Jewish adoptive families.

Tout Timoun Nou Yo (All Our Children)
5793 Turtle Lake Rd
Shoreview MN 55126
612-920-3149
4 pgs, US$7/yr.
Newsletter on Haitian adoptions.

Trying Times
19605-J S. State Road 7, #139
Boca Raton FL 33498
6/yr, US$19.95/yr.
Newsletter on infertility and adoption options.

Wide Smiles
Joanne Green, Editor
Box 5153
Stockton CA 95205
Quarterly, US$18/yr.
Newsletter on cleft lip and palate.

Working Smart
SMA Info Services
5929-149th Ave SE
Bellevue WA 98006
206-643-6136; FAX 747-1296
Quarterly, US$15/yr, includes membership in SMA-Adopt
Subtitled "A newsletter of tips and techniques for the adoptive parent".

Index by Publisher or Editor

Fédération des Parents adoptants du Québec: *FPAQ Newsletter*
Forget Me Not Family Society: *Adoption Circles*

Gage, William L.: *Adoptionsdreieck; Geborener Deutscher*
Green, Joanne: *Wide Smiles*
Group of Adoptive Parents: *GAP Newsletter*
Groves, Pamela: *Growing with FAS*

Infertility Awareness Assn of Canada: *Infertility Awareness*
International Adoption Families Group: *IAFG Newsletter*
International Concerns Committee for Children (ICCC): *ICCC Newsletter*
International Social Service Canada: *ISS Canada Newsletter*

Jones, Katherin: *Adoption Helper*

Kim, Douglas: *Cousins*
KinQuest Inc.: *Quest*

Latin America Parents Assn (LAPA): *Buenas Noticias, Que Tal*
Latin American Adoptive Families (LAAF): *LAAF Quarterly*
Latin America Adoptive Families (LAAF) In Canada: *LAAF News*

Melina, Lois: *Adopted Child*
Moncton Adoptive Parents Assn (MAPA): *MAPA Newsletter*

National Adoption Center (NAC): *NAC News*
National Adoption Information Clearinghouse (NAIC): *National Adoption Directory*
National Assn for Perinatal Addiction Research: *Perinatal Addiction Research and Education Update*
National Coalition to End Racism in America's Child Care System: *Children's Voice*
National Council For Adoption: *National Adoption Reports*
National Resource Center for Special Needs Adoption: *Roundtable*
Neuberger, Sondra: *AdoptNet Magazine*
North American Council on Adoptable Children: *Adoptalk*
Nova Scotia Adoptive Parents Assn (NSAPA): *NSAPA Newsletter*

Open Door Society: *ODS News*
Opportunities for Latin American Children: *OLA Ninos Newsletter*

PACT—An Adoption Alliance, Inc.: *PACT Press*
Parent Finders Inc.: *PFI Communiqué*
Parent Finders: *Parent Finders (National Capital Region) Newsletter*
Parents for Private Adoption (PPA): *PPA Newsletter*
Parents of Peruvian Adoptees: *Dear P.O.P.A.*
Peck, Cynthia: *Roots and Wings*

Rapone, Anita: *Guatemalan North-American Families Newsletter*
Romania Children's Connection (RCC): *RCC Newsletter*

Saskatchewan Adoptive Parents Assn (SAPA): *SAPA News*
Schmidt, Debbie: *Families for Children Newsletter No. 2*
Search Institute: *Adoptive Families Update, Source*
Single Parent Adoption Support Group: *SPA Newsletter*
SMA Info Services: *Working Smart*
Society of Special Needs Adoptive Parents (SNAP): *SNAP Newsletter*
Stars of David International Inc.: *Star Tracks*
Support For Parents Adopting and Raising World Kids: *Sparks*

Troy, Andrea: *NY Singles Adopting Children*

U.S. Chilean Adoptive Families: *Copihue*

Vancouver Infertility Peer Support Group (VIPS): *VIPS Newsletter*

WAIF: *FYI*
Walton, Gail: *Connections; Namaste Newsletter*

Much of the information set out in this appendix was supplied by the newsletter *Adoption Helper*.

appendix • • • • • • • • • • • • • • III

Adoption Books and Studies

The following is a list of the adoption books and studies that I found interesting. There are many other good resources. The Toronto newsletter *Adoption Helper* will supply you with an adoption bibliography for two dollars. A free guide to adoption-related literature can be obtained from William Lewis Gage.

Adoption Helper
189 Springdale Blvd.
Toronto, Ont. M4C 1Z6

William Lewis Gage
805 Alvarado Drive N.E.
Albuquerque, N.M. 87108

General Adoption Issues

Daly, Kerry J. and Michael P. Sobol. *Adoption in Canada.* Guelph, Ontario: National Adoption Study, University of Guelph, 1993.
> The conclusions of a study on key adoption trends, existing adoption policy and legislation, the factors associated with pregnancy decision making and the provision of adoption services in Canada.

Gilman, Lois. *The Adoption Resource Book.* New York: HarperCollins Publishers, 1984, 1987, 1992.
> Terrific resource book. Examines the various methods of adoption, preparing for a child and then raising that child.

Samuels, Shirley C. *Ideal Adoption: A Comprehensive Guide to Forming an Adoptive Family.* New York: Plenum Press, 1990.
> Gives a brief description of the various issues in adoption.

Sorosky, Arthur D. and Annette Baran and Reuben Pannor. *The Adoption Triangle— Sealed or Opened Records: How They Affect Adoptees, Birth Parents, and Adoptive Parents.* San Antonio: Corona Publishing Co., 1978, 1989.
> Discusses the need to open adoption records. Contains a good review of the history of adoption.

Infertility Resolution

Johnston, Patricia Irwin. *Adopting After Infertility*. Indianapolis: Perspectives Press, 1992.
> Great. An insightful guide through infertility resolution and the learning stage of adoption.

_____. *Taking Charge of Infertility*. Indianapolis: Perspectives Press, 1994.
> An expansion of the infertility resolution discussions contained in *Adopting After Infertility*.

Salzer, Linda P. *Surviving Infertility: A Compassionate Guide through the Emotional Crisis of Infertility*. New York: HarperCollins Publishers, 1986, 1991.
> Title says it best.

The Adoption Process

Hicks, Randall B. *Adopting in America: How to Adopt Within One Year*. Sun City, California: Wordslinger Press, 1993.
> A guide to private adoption written by a lawyer specializing in adoption. Contains a summary of the laws of each U.S. state.

Martin, Cynthia D. *Beating the Adoption Game*. Orlando: Harvest Brace Jovanovich, 1988.
> A comprehensive manual to the adoption process.

Reynolds, Nancy Thalia. *Adopting Your Child*. Vancouver: Self-Counsel Press, 1993.
> Helps you steer yourself through the adoption learning process. Contains a chapter on "How Canadians can adopt in and through the United States."

Special-Needs Adoption

Dunn, Linda (editor). *Adopting Children with Special Needs: A Sequel*. North American Council on Adoptable Children, 1983.
> A series of short discussions on various special needs from different perspectives.

Jewett, Claudia L. *Adopting the Older Child*. Harvard, Mass.: Harvard Common Press, 1978.
> A wonderful book that follows the stories of several children and their adoptive families.

Nelson, Katherine A. *On the Frontier of Adoption: A Study of Special-Needs Adoptive Families*. Washington: Child Welfare League of America, 1985.
> The conclusions of a study examining the problems faced by those adopting special-needs children.

International Adoption

Bartholet, Elizabeth. *Family Bonds: Adoption and The Politics of Parenting*. New York: Houghton Mifflin, 1993.
> Intertwined in the details of Bartholet's adoption of two children born in Peru are her thought-provoking critiques of society's adoption practices.

Bowen, John. *A Canadian Guide to International Adoptions: How to Find, Adopt, and Bring Home Your Child*. North Vancouver: Self-Counsel Press, 1992.
> A practical guide to adopting a child born outside of Canada.

Register, Cheri. *Are Those Kids Yours? American Families with Children Adopted from Other Countries*. New York: The Free Press, A Division of Macmillan, Inc., 1991.
> Very good. A complete and realistic discussion about the issues involved in an international adoption.

Westhues, Anne and Joyce S. Cohen. *Intercountry Adoption in Canada*. Final Report. January 1994. Funded by National Welfare Grants, Human Resources Development Canada.
> The conclusions of a study on how internationally adopted children and their families fare when the child has reached adolescence.

Openness in Adoption

Arms, Suzanne. *Adoption: A Handful of Hope.*
New York: Knopf, 1990.
Revised edition of the 1983 book, *To
Love and Let Go*, profiling birth parents,
adoptive parents and adoptees.

Caplin, Lincoln. *An Open Adoption.* New
York: Farrar, Straus and Giroux, 1990.
A general discussion about open adoption
is weaved throughout the story of one
particular open adoption.

Gritter, James L. (editor). *Adoption Without
Fear.* San Antonio: Corona, 1989.
A handful of adoptive parents who
worked with the same agency tell their
open adoption stories.

McRoy, Ruth and Harold Grotevant. *Openness
in Adoption: New Practices, New Issues.* New
York: Praeger, 1988.
Preliminary conclusions of a study on
openness in adoption. Based on interview
data from seventeen adoptive families and
birth parents. Contains a good summary
of the literature on open adoption.

Melina, Lois Ruskai and Sharon Kaplan
Roszia. *The Open Adoption Experience.* New
York: Harper Perennial, 1993.
Terrific. "A complete guide for adoptive
and birth families—from making the
decision through the child's growing
years."

Rappaport, Bruce M. *The Open Adoption
Book: A Guide to Adoption without Tears.*
New York: MacMillan Publishing Company,
1992.
An adoption agency director focuses on
prospective adoptive parents' fears about
open adoption.

Silber, Kathleen and Phyllis Speedlin. *Dear
Birthmother.* San Antonio: Corona, 1990.
Revised edition of the 1982 book that
introduced opening adoptions by
exchanging letters between birth and
adoptive families.

Sibler, Kathleen and Patricia Martinez Dorner.
Children of Open Adoption. San Antonio:
Corona, 1989.
Using case studies, examines the effect of
an open adoption on a number of children.

Parenting Adopted Children

Cohen, Nancy J. and James Duvall and
James C. Coyne. *Mental Health Service
Needs of Post-Adoptive Families.* Final Report.
January 1994. Funded by National Welfare
Grants, Health & Welfare Canada.
The conclusions of a study on mental
health service needs of post-adoptive
families.

Melina, Lois. *Raising Adopted Children: A
Manual for Adoptive Parents.* New York:
Harper & Row, 1986.
A very interesting review of the various
issues that adoptive parents must
understand and manage.

Melina, Lois Ruskai. *Making Sense of
Adoption: A Parent's Guide.* New York:
Harper & Row Publishers, 1989.
Uses sample conversations and suggested
activities to help adoptive parents
communicate with their children.

Schaffer, Judith and Christina Lindstrom.
How to Raise an Adopted Child. New York:
Crown, 1989.
A resource book on various parenting
issues.

Siegel, Stephanie. *Parenting Your Adopted
Child: A Complete and Loving Guide.* New
York: Prentice Hall Press, 1989.
A simple guide containing several
interesting parenting discussions.

Adoption Theory and Philosophy (scholarly works)

Brodzinsky, David and Marshall Schechter
(editors). *The Psychology of Adoption.* New
York: Oxford University Press, 1990.
Several essays by researchers on the
issues faced by the parties to an adoption.

Brodzinsky, David, Marshall Schechter and Robin Marantz Henig. *Being Adopted: The Lifelong Search for Self*. New York: Doubleday, 1992.
    Uses the reflections of adoptees to trace how adoption is experienced over a lifetime.

Daly, Kerry J.E. *Becoming Adoptive Parents: Shifts in Identity from Biological Parenthood to Adoptive Parenthood Among Infertile Couples*. Ottawa: National Library of Canada, 1988. [6 microfiche] Thesis Ph.D. McMaster University, 1987.
    Findings of a study showing there can be a concurrent commitment to both biological and adoptive parenthood.

Kirk, H. David. *Shared Fate: A Theory and Method of Adoptive Relationships*. Brentwood Bay, B.C.: Ben-Simon Publishers, 1964, 1984.
    Discusses the effect of adoption on the family. Stresses that parenting by adoption is different from parenting by birth.

Rosenberg, Elinor B. *The Adoption Life Cycle: The Children and Their Families through the Years*. New York: Free Press, 1992.
    Reviews the psychological aspects of each member of the adoption triad: the birth parents, the adoptive parents and the adoptee.

Index

J

May 29/95